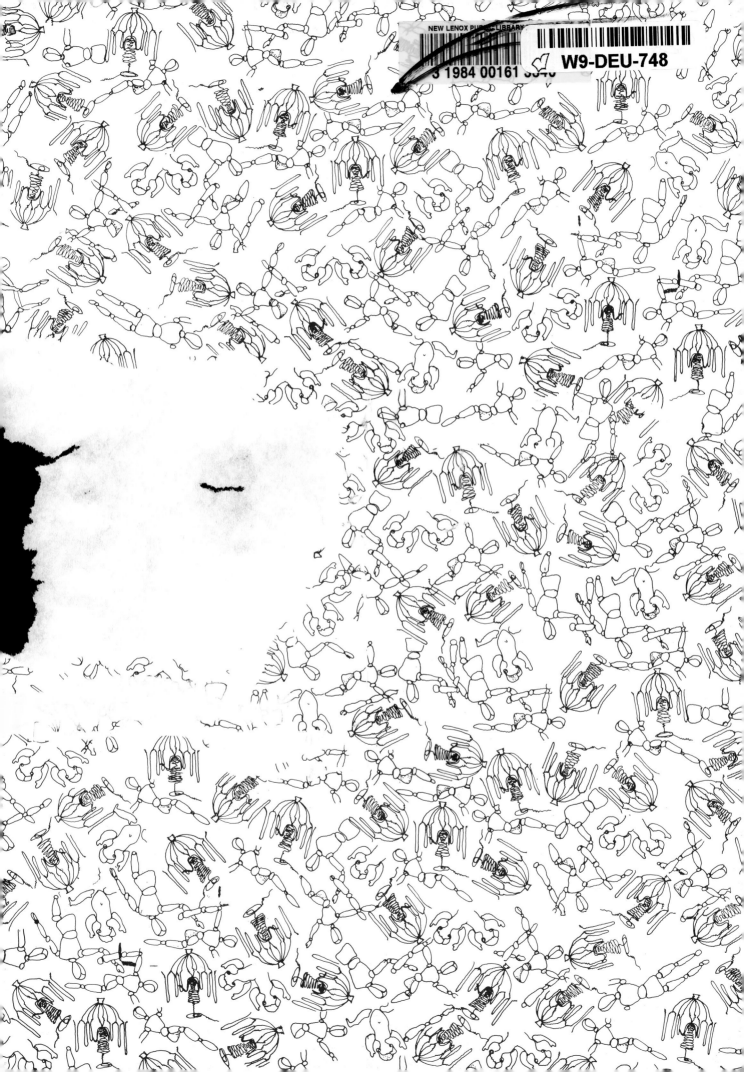

# THE TWENTIETH CENTURY
# HISTORIES OF FASHION

Series edited by
Ieri Attualità

THE TWENTIETH CENTURY
FASHION AND DRESS
Tentative titles

WOMAN

1. Evening dresses 1900 ... 1940 (Marco Tosa)
2. Evening dresses 1940 ... (Marco Tosa)
3. Maternity fashion (Doretta Davanzo Poli)
4. Skirts & more skirts (Flora Gandolfi)
5. Costume jewellery
6. Shoes for special occasions
7. Details: sleeves
8. Strictly personal: corsets and brassières
9. Petticoats & co.
10. Nightwear
11. Trousers for women
12. Day and evening bags
13. Blouses
14. Large and small hats
15. Hosiery and related items
16. Gloves
17. Cloaks and coats
18. Light coats and raincoats
19. Accessories for ladies: umbrellas and canes
20. Hairstyles
21. You can do anything with fur vol. 1
22. You can do anything with fur vol. 2
23. Casual shoes and boots
24. Afternoon and cocktail dresses
25. Shawls, scarfs and silk squares
26. Bridal gowns
27. Work-clothes
28. Beachwear and swimsuits
29. Details: necks and necklines
30. Belts and artificial flowers
31. Suits and daywear
32. Tricot and jersey fashions

CHILDREN

33. Children in their party dress (Nora Villa)
34. Girls
35. Children and brats
36. Children's shoes
37. Teenage boys
38. Teenage girls
39. Babies

MEN

40. Men's hats (Giuliano Folledore)
41. Furs for Men (Anna Municchi)
42. Trousers & co. (Vittoria de Buzzaccarini)
43. Work-clothes
44. Underwear
45. Shirts
46. Men's accessories: belts, gloves, ties and scarfs
47. Jackets
48. Waistcoats
49. Men's jewellery
50. Raincoats, ponchos and k-ways
51. Umbrellas, sticks and canes
52. Overcoats and coats
53. Pyjamas, robes etc.
54. Knitwear: cardigans and pullovers
55. Sportswear
56. Hairstyles, beards and mustaches
57. Shoes and boots
58. Uniforms
59. Suitcases, briefcases and bags
60. Swimsuits
61. Casualwear: blouson jackets and cabans

SPECIAL ITEMS

62. The handkerchief
63. Buttons
64. Ribbons round the world
65. Leather clothing
66. Jeans
67. T- and polo shirt
68. Glasses

FABRICS

69. Fabrics in fashions: cotton
70. Fabrics in fashions: wool
71. Fabrics in fashions: silk
72. Fabrics in fashions: man-made fabrics

NORA VILLA

# Children in Their Party Dress

**Zanfi** Editori

ACKNOWLEDGEMENTS

The author would like to thank for their help:
Kirsten Aschengreen Piacenti of the Galleria del
Costume di Palazzo Pitti;
Silvana Bernasconi,
Silvio Belekda,
Laura Biagiotti,
Bianca Brichetto,
Paola Brichetto Guida,
Marina Fenghi,
Sorelle Fontana,
Silvia Mattoni,
Studio Moschino,
Adriana Montorsi,
Alessandro Savella,
Igor and Raffaello Uboldi


PHOTOGRAPHIC CREDITS

Pictures on page 7, 11, 12, 13 are from the
collection of Silvana Bernasconi.
Photographs by Betty Brunelli.

Photographs on page 28, 29, 37, 38, 64, 65, 66, 68,
83, 84, 85 are from the Biblioteca del Centro Studi di
Storia del Tessuto e del Costume, Palazzo
Mocenigo, Venezia. Photographs by Giacomelli.

Drawings n. 140, 141, 142, 143 are by Fiora Gandolfi.

All other illustrations are from the author's private
and Ieri Attualità archives.
Photographs by Giuliano Grossi and Ivano Medici.

Coordination: Vittoria de Buzzaccarini
Editorial staff: Vittoria de Buzzaccarini,
Elena Vezzalini
Iconographic research: for Ieri Attualità
Chiara Padovano and Giuseppe Pellissetti;
Nora Villa
Graphic design: Giorgio Trani
Cover: Studio Cancelli
Translation: Donna R. Miller
Original title: Bambini vestiti a festa

© 1989 ||||| Zanfi Editori s.r.l.
Via Ganaceto 121, 41100 Modena (Italy)
Tel. 059/222292 - Telefax 059/225719
Telex 214614 Zanfi I

ISBN 88-85168-46-9

Il Novecento
Periodico - Aut. Trib. di Modena n. 904 del 18/01/88
Sped. abb. post. GR. III/70
Publisher: Celestino Zanfi

# INDEX

*...to Igor and Raffaello*

# A CHILDREN'S STORY

1.

**1.** Portrait of an aristocratic child decked out in the family clothes and jewels which were passed down from generation to generation, 17th century Spanish school. Anon. Silvana Bernasconi Collection.

## WHEN CLOTHES WERE ALWAYS 'SUNDAY-BEST'

The history of children's ceremonial clothing went hand in hand for centuries with that of adult manners and customs. Indeed, children's clothing received what amounted to very little attention, not least because it was considered more a reflection of grown-up tastes and requirements than an expression of those of the children themselves. The history of their formal dress is, of course, the history of their attire *tout court* since the writings and paintings which have come down to us testify almost solely to the fashions of the children of those who counted. If normal people were all but neglected, the lowest classes were ignored.

And this is the way things were until several decades ago when children came into their own, so to speak. Since then, children's rights, have been pushed further and further by economic interests which fast rivalled traditional adult ones - in the toy sector, the fashion sector and, yes, the educational sector as well.

The revolution had begun long before of course - back in the Enlightenment with John Locke and Jean Jacques Rousseau. It then continued in the nineteenth-century with Pestalozzi and down to present day twentieth-century education with Montessori. But back then, with dynasties to safeguard and political alliances to weave, children were weighed down with responsibilities long before their time. Their gold brocades and fine laces may well seem to us a sort of compensation for such premature worries, a way of making up for those practically unknown carefree joys of childhood wich had to be sacrificed for one's family or the State. These were clothes which designated one's social class and these were times in which life expectancy was low, and *carpe diem* was the motto. The future Peter the Great came to the throne when he was but ten and Louis XIV but five, while Vittoria della Rovere was officially engaged to the future Ferdinand II of Tuscany when she was only twenty months old and still in diapers!

P'u Yi, the last emperor of China, is a recent example. He came to the throne in 1908, when he was two. At his coronation he

**2.3.** P'u Yi, the last emperor of China, crowned in 1908 at the age of two: the official photograph and a still from Bertolucci's 1987 movie version.

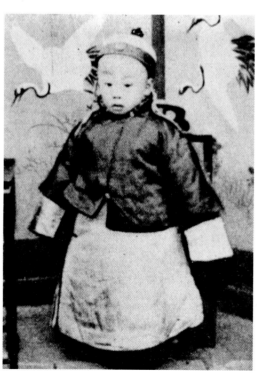

2.

3.

8

was decked out in high platform slippers, embroidered trousers and tunic and sported a Mongul fur and gold head-covering.

## SO VERY GENTEEL...

We start to come out of those early, mysterious Dark Ages with the elegant dress of the 1200s. The tendency to flaunt one's riches in one's children's style of dress was fast coming into vogue, so much so that Bologna's sumptuary laws were emended to regulate how much could be spent on each sleeve of clothing for males up to twelve and still-unmarried females! In the 1200s, a Renaissance began to flower. The rise of the city-states or communes after the year 1000 opened up all sorts of new opportunities for the artisan. In a town like Florence small shops belonging to goldsmiths, painters, wool merchants, tailors and so on began to spring up literally all over the place. In his "*Cronaca*", Dino Compagni tells us of "fabulous houses teeming with necessary arts". And it is here in this Florence that Dante meets his Beatrice at the tender age of nine. As he recounts in his *Vita Nova*, "She was dressed in the most patrician of colors, a subdued and decorous crimson, her robe bound round and adorned in a style suitable to her years," (trans, M. Musa, Indiana U P, 1973). It is not hard for us to picture her dressed elegantly, beautifully - not least because children of noble families did not go out dressed in any other way.

## THE PAGES

During the 1300s, this habit of providing one's children with few but excellent things to wear becomes widespread. Towards the end of the century, elegant cloth stockings which are held up by a belt arrive on the scene. Made of colours which were bright, lively and even different per leg, these gave the adolescent wearer an air of light-hearted distinction. Over these, a short tunic coming down to mid-thigh is worn. Two strips of material hang from the shoulders which are vaguely reminiscent of the leading strings used to teach a child to walk. The finishing touches to the outfit worn by the palace and

4. A page in tunic and stockings. A. Mantegna. Detail of *Camera degli Sposi*, Mantua.

court pages were a shoulder-length hair style and a tapering head-dress to top it off.

In the frescoes of the Medici-Riccardi chapel in Florence, the painter Benozzo Gossoli goes so far as to make a profane point on the sacred pretext of the Nativity. He has depicted even the folds and creases of the hose worn by the pages in the entourage of the Magi, merely to render more exquisitely the sumptuousness of 15th-century Florentine life.

The widespread habit at the time of sending one's sons off to be pages can be likened to the nineteenth-century custom of sending them off to boarding schools. The local lord's generosity in taking the boy on, however, did not include the trappings he was expected to don. John Paston, a young English page to the Duke of Norfolk in 1465, wrote his mother begging her to pick up two pair of stockings from the famous hosiers located near Black Friars' Gate, one black and one scarlet, "I pray my mother not to forget since, no longer in possession of a pair in one piece, I am in desperate need." wrote this poor if honored page, adding, "please pay the bill which amounts to three shillings for me as well."

## PORTRAIT OF AN ERA AND OF A STATUS-SYMBOL

In the 1500s clothing elegance reaches its peak. New styles led to a rigidly defined and regulated dress code which was increasingly viewed as a status symbol. Clothes-making techniques themselves improved with the invention of modern scissors, the use of the thimble and the advent of buttons and metal button-holes. The Courts, their lords and their children, began to vie with each other in extravagant ways, which meant that the descendants of the VIPs had to become walking advertisements for their family's wealth and power, much as house furnishings - paintings, ceramics, knick-knacks - had always been. These too-gorgeous children were then immortalized by the court painters.

These pictures then toured the major courts of Europe, sent as they were by means of ambassadors to noble relatives or others of like rank of the other royal houses. Such gifts were an attempt to form or strengthen dynastic ties through marriages and were a pledge of such alliances. There they hung, on the walls of the picture galleries of the sovereigns of Europe, who would occasionally peruse the faces of these children in search of a husband or wife for their own.

## MORE SALIENT DETAILS...

Even those with no blue blood running in their veins were able to don what resembled a doctor's white coat - a sort of full, knee-length coat which was sleeveless so that the elegant puffed sleeves of the justaucorps could be seen. Hair was worn very short and tapered at the temples. As a head-covering,

5.

6.

a beretta with a feather cocked in the side would do quite well.

For concerto or theater-going, the little girls at Court learned to wear the vertugade, with its full, stiff, wooden or metal, bell-shaped hoops, as soon as they could walk. Over this cage-like structure, two or three stiffly starched petticoats were worn and, over those, the precious outer skirt woven through with real gold or silver. The bodices were tight and made rigid with metal or whale-bone stays, coming down below the waistline proper and over the skirt into a kind of pointed "V"-effect. A fine, lace-trimmed apron was then worn over the girls" ceremonial dress - a detail which will come down through the mawkish late eighteenth century and into the strict nineteenth when it will come to be a quasi-symbol of the virtues of the future house-wife.

## CHILDREN'S ROLE-PLAYING

In the century of the Baroque, male and female children began to be dressed differently from the age of about six or seven. The outfits are two-piece: trousers and jerkin for the boys and skirt and bodice for the girls. Up to then, both were dressed in long skirts and stiff corselets. in such upright splendour the young Medicis, Farneses and the

**5.** A noble descendant in the "sculpted" fashion of the 15th century. The cod-piece was a symbol of virility worn by all males from a very early age. S. Coello, *Arciduca Wenzel*, Vienna.

**6.** 17th century Spanish *Infante costume*. D. Velasquez, *Infante Balthazar Carlos*, Vienna.

**7.8.** Up to the age of around seven, both males and females were dressed in long skirts. The only difference: a frilly cap for the girls. D. Velasquez, *Il Principe Felipe Prospero* Vienna. Dutch, 14th century, Silvana Bernasconi Collection.

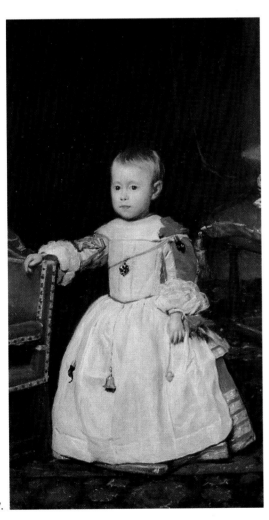

7.

8.

descendants of the Roveres were painted, the only sign of gender distinction being a rose or doll in hand for a girl and a side-worn sword for a boy.

Round about the beginning of the eighteenth century, the boys begin to wear three-piece outfits composed of tight breeches, string-tied below the knee, a waistcoat which went over a silk muslin shirt and a knee-length justaucorps with cuffs. A tie - a light-weight bit of material, silk embroidered or edged in lace, falling from the shirt collar like a *jabot* and thick-heeled shoes complete the picture. The Louis XIV style of heavy, curled wig gave way to a much lighter kind, powdered, gathered at the neck and tied back with a velvet bow. That symbol of the rocoò, the three-cornered hat, was carried about superciliously by children whose wigs were simply too voluminous for them to fit! In such guise, the infant prodigy, Mozart, gave his first concerts at the Courts of Europe - amid the general applause of the public and his father's grumbling.

In the latter half of the eighteenth century we witness the desire to dress male children up, not so much according to what they were but in view of what they were to become, or rather what their parents had decided they were soon to be, given the high rate of infant mortality of the times. The majorat system, by which the first-born son inherited the family title and riches, was still in practice and therefore the other brothers were often willingly trained for other careers. As a result, it was not uncommon to see these younger boys, once out of their skirts, trapsing about the palace salons as though dressed up for a costume party, disguided as priests or abbots with their crimson silk, rustling cassocks or garbed like miniature cavalry soldiers, but in any case wearing both the clothes and air of the role they would most likely be playing in later life, like it or not...

## THE PRINCIPLES OF PEDAGOGY

It was the Englishman, John Locke, philosopher and educator, who cast the first stones at the rigid and hampering regulations governing children's education in his *Thoughts on Education* of 1695, not failing to include among his targets the current fashion of dressing them. Jean

9.

Jacques Rousseau added his voice seventy years later with his novel *Emile*, 1762, in which he suggests new methods for raising and educating children. A light could now be glimpsed at the end of this suffocating, dark tunnel, "Infancy must be cherished", Rouseau affirms polemically, "Children have a right to their happiness, to give free rein to their instincts, to play". His words sound revolutionary if we consider the indifference, if not downright tyranny or complete denial of affection, hitherto practiced by adults with regard to their offspring. Regarding specifically the question of dress, there are certain pages of Rousseau's that come across as a virtual *manifesto*: "Emile must be able to run, to play outdoors with his head uncovered. He must wear loose clothing that does not bind his weak chest or crush his lungs".

And from that point on, indeed, for the very first time, children's fashions begin to take on a new identity, their own identity. Very soon, specialized children's tailors and dressmakers were to come up with a new kind of overall whose trousers were no longer fastened below the knee. Rather they were ankle-length, wide , and actually comfortable! Above, there was a loose-fitting bodice modelled on the English

12

**9.10.11.** In the mid-17th century, younger sons were still dressed according to the role they were supposed to assume later on in life, while the girls' precious lacy apron presages adult femininity. Italy, 15th century; France, 16th century. Silvana Bernasconi Collection.

peasant-style, long-sleeved smock, attached to the trousers with the fewest number of buttons possible. The new look called for white or light-colored cotton fabrics that would be strong and play-resistant. The elegant versions of the same style were made up of taffeta or shot silk velvets. The children staring forth from the portraits of this epoque's greatest painters certainly appear to be a lot happier than their predecessors.

The little girls who had the honour of being allowed to come into Lady Mother's *boudoir* for a short time once a day resembled nothing so much as brightly wrapped sweets in their floor-length, soft and frilly, snow-white muslin gowns with a colored silk band wound round their waists. Gone are the stiff corsets and petticoats, as are the wigs. Hair is now worn short. Stockings are white and shoes light-weight and adorned with attractive buckles, Moreover, from the mid-1700s onwards, people begin to appreciate the merits of a

good, wholesome bath and the children's lightened elegance is given a freshening up as well.

## THE BOURGEOIS AND VICTORIAN CENTURY

Following the rumbles of revolution and the imperial glories of the Bonaparte era, the bourgeoisie, now released from their fixation for imitating aristocratic customs, develop a life style that is comfortable, respectable and highly prudish, a set of values summed up in their lofty sentiments towards "the family". And thus the clocks are turned back. Little girls' skirts are once again blown up, though they have been shortened to lower calf-length to reveal the *ruche* and flounce of their long bloomers. The boys' long trousers are worn with short, matching jackets in the style of what would become the official uniform of the most exclusive English public school, Eton. Bright colors soon gave way to dull grey. The jacket was extremely short and pointed behind, "spencer" style. The collar was rounded, white and starched stiff. And the short boots were either tied up with laces or had elastic straps at the sides. Even once the top hat had been given up, this remained the elegant, ceremonial attire of the children of the middle and upper classes right up to the eve of World War II.

For a good deal of the nineteenth century, all talk of children's freedom was forgotten. In the Victorian drawing room of the latter half of the century, a poker-faced governess would typically be seen tightly holding on to the hands of the children come down to pay their respects with a bow or curtsy to the adult world - as well as they could, of course, given their stiff, starched clothing.

And it was dressed in this same way that the bon ton children of Humbert's Italy

14

**12.** Two children prettily dressed for a family party. *La Mode Illustrée,* 1867.

15.

performed their own reverant bows to their grown-up world, while in Austria they kissed the hands of grandmothers and maiden aunts or grasped each other's white-gloved hands, bending their heads to hide embarrassed giggles when the dancing teacher measured the beat of a quadrille or waltz.

Towards the end of the 1860s, girls' crinoline goes out of fashion but is often replaced (and quite early on in these girls' careers) with those absurdly extravagant

**13.** Boy's elegant velvet suit with silk sash. *Illustrierte Frauen Zeitung,* 1889.

**14.** A ceremonial dress for a little girl of the drawing rooms. *La Novità,* 1878.

**15.16.** Party fashions for nineteenth-century children were extremely smart but hardly suitable for rough play with all those crinolin petticoats and whatnot. *La Mode Illustrée,* 1887.

15

**16.**

bustles worn behind, at the base of the spine: the *cul de Paris*, as someone called them in tribute to their place of origin. But progress continued to be made in one way or another, thanks to the combined efforts of those doctors, teachers and parents having a bit of good sense. In the second half of the nineteenth century in England, the movement takes the form of the Rational Dress Society (1881), the product of a by then widespread campaign for freedom of dress - and cleanliness.

**17.** An intimate family after-dinner concert on New Year's Eve. The girl in a dress embroidered in broderie anglaise and the boy dressed as the perfect little violinist in a velvet suit with a fancy collar vaguely reminiscent of the sailor suit. *La Saison,* 1899.

16

17.

# THE TWENTIETH CENTURY AND THE *BELLE EPOQUE*

## A DECLARATION OF RIGHTS

The turn of the century is marked by a formal declaration by law-makers that this was to be the century of the child. Clearly, however, such an assertion - categoric and binding as it may have been believed - is never enough. Neither the family nor society at large can be said to be really prepared to give children the autonomy they require.

The first decade of the new century in Italy is a relatively stable time combining the last frothy waves of the *Belle Epoque* with the sinuous scrolls of *art nouveau*.

All over Europe, the process of industrialization which was to make even Italy a modern nation is well under way. Thanks to the inventions of the previous century - Isaac Singer's sewing machine, button-holing and attaching machines and Barran's cutter - the U.S., England and Germany were able to set up their first companies for the mass production of clothing. The new controlled cost

**18.** This rare photo of Gabriele D'Annunzio was taken when the divine poet was about three or four. As can be seen, the custom of dressing little boys in skirts was still in vogue.

18.

Naples to Rome and sets up a small store and atelier for the making of children's clothes. In a very few years the business grows to the point of taking up, window after window, the whole building in Via della Maddalena and in 1917 he earns himself the title of "Purveyor to the Royal House". The most tradition-bound European families, however, prefer to order their children's things from London, choosing them from a catalogue published once a year in September.

19.

manufacturing was applied to the men's fashion sector and, in England, to that of children's wear. Up till the mid-1800s, shoes and clothes were exclusively the product of artisans but now industry and handicrafts begin to learn peaceful coexistence, although the rich bourgeoisie still run off to the best tailors and dressmakers to have their clothes made. At the very start of the new century Gennaro Zingone moves from

20.

19

21.

**19.** This girl's pink silk dress is made even more sumptuous by the addition of a large lace macramé collar, a low-waisted sash and decorative rose. *La Mode Illustrée*, January 25, 1903.

**20.** The sailor-suit was already the elegant little boys' outfit by the end of the nineteenth century. *La Mode Illustrée*, September 16, 1900.

**21.** The Savoia family children's wear is pure white, lace-decorated and embroidered, as was fitting for the official photographs of the Italian Royal family. Baby Prince Humbert (in his mother's arms) is wearing the customary little white dress. 1905.

## THE ENGLISH STYLE: A 'MUST' FOR ALL OCCASIONS

Hogson Burnett's "Little Lord Fauntleroy" becomes the model of the most popular boys' look from the first decades of the twentieth century onwards. The name comes from the famous nineteenth century sentimental novel about a little lord whose great burden of worries ends up stifling any of the childhood joys he should have had. The suit was made of blue wool. The calf-length trousers went with a slightly flared jacket coming down right beneath the waistline, with a sole cloth-covered button fixed at the neckline, right below the rounded collar that often sported a bit of lace which in turn was fixed to the silk or white linen cambric shirt with small buttons. The main sign of the children's fashion times was undoubtedly the ever-shorter trousers' length. It even made it easier for hand-me-downs to be made to fit younger brother. It

is rather amusing to think of the problems that arose when the responsibility for dressing cousin Ferdinand, ingored by both busy parents and governess, fell to his grandmother on his father's side! The dear old thing, still under the influence of the ways of the traditional Habsburg bon ton *fin de siècle*, insisted on dressing the poor youth up in blue calf-length trousers with the old-fashioned two buttons, even though boys had been wearing elegant knee-length suit trousers for ten years or so!

But there is another fashion that arrives from England and fast becomes the European child's classic elegant dress - both for males and females alike. This was the "sailor-suit", first sported in the 1870s by Edward, the little Prince of Wales, whether of his own accord or because he had been convinced somehow of its merits, we will, of course, never know. In any case, the long trousers and classic blousy top were made of gabardine, of wool and of, fittingly, "navy"

20

22.        23.        24.        25.

blue cloth. The neckline falls into a large square collar in the back and, for the elegant version of the model, is usually made of silk and edged with two rows of thin white silk cord having two bits of symmetrical white trimming in either corner - military five point stars or admirals' anchors usually. The collar, coming down the front into a point, is fixed with a simple but elegant loop. The girls' version features a white skirt whose continuous tiny knife-pleats are gathered up and attached to the waist band itself or sewn below, at a distance of fifteen centimeters from the waist, or perhaps even start off from a basque in order to avoid unsightly bunching-up beneath the cassock top. Long, black stockings and glossy, high-laced, black patent leather shoes complete the outfit.

**22.-25.** Various versions of the classic sailor suit for boys and girls alike. The fashion will periodically make its reappearance on and off all during the twentieth century. *La Mode Pratique,* 1906; *La Saison,* 1900; *Illustrierte Frauen Zeitung,* 1889.

**26.** Two future Kings of England wearing their white cotton sailor suits. Prince Albert (later, George VI), with his grandfather King Edward VII and Prince Edward (Edward VIII) at Sandrigham, 1901.

**26.**

## THE DRAWING ROOMS
## OF EUROPE

It is almost as though Paris and London sat down and divided the fashion world in two, each taking half for their own sphere of influence. Out of Paris came the dicta for women's fashions, while London laid down the rules for the men and children.

Victorian England, after the great queen's death, gave way to the Edwardian era. The changes were many, but not all for the best.. The almost fanatical respectability and politeness of Victoria's years were watered down with more than a dash of hypocrisy.

In the drawing rooms of England and those of republican France, in Vittorio Emanuele III's Italy and the ever more Habsburg (and mournful) Austria, children - suitably and formally stiffened up - continue to be admitted to the presence of their elders only on special occasions. Victoria still reigned over children's fashions. Little boys and girls both still wore long skirts up till the age of about four. In his autobiography *A Sort of Life*, Graham Green, who was born in 1904, gives us a picture of himself and the times: "I was about four and wore a skirt and little bib. My hair hung in ringlets down to my shoulders..."

The dress of the host of governesses, easy-going nannies and nursemaids takes on an elegance of its own: wide skirts with several petticoats underneath; white, starched linen blouses and gathered ruffles; amber and coral necklaces and a head-square fixed into a chignon at the nape of the neck with a pair of silver filigree hair pins. Such was the garb of the woman in whose arms these children made their rare if triumphant appearances to be cooed over by mother's friends and relatives and all those people gathered together to perform their social duties with an indulgent smile, a bit of gossip and a cup of tea.

27.

28.

**27.** A photo of a child with his nanny from the family album. 1900.

**28.** Embroidered white linen cambric dress with lace insertion - for the tender years. *Illustrierte Frauen Zeitung*, 1898.

**29.** Turn of the century brother and sister pose for a snapshot in their look-alike embroidered white linen dresses.

## CHURCH GOING

In a Catholic country like Italy, a child's life was one religious celebration after another, marked off by a string of sacramental rites, beginning with Baptism. The christening dress got handed down from one generation to another in any self-respecting family. As can be imagined, they were adorned with lace, with precious silk embroidery or, more simply, with linen cambric around which shiny, starched embroidered frills tumbled down. The child was placed upon a cushion which had been specially shaped and covered to match the dress in material and decorations. This was known as the *porte-enfant* and was carried into the church by father, accompanied by all the members of the family and the godmother and godfather, who had been chosen from among them. The only one missing was mother, who was still enjoying her post-childbirth rest. Covered in lace herself and stretched out on a couch, a chaise longue or perhaps still propped up in bed, she awaited her newly baptised baby's return from the ceremony so that its health and that of the lucky parents could be suitably toasted.

Even in humblest of families, Baptism was celebrated with the decorum befitting a sacrament. The child's dress was made of white cotton in honeycomb patterned piqué or in muslin. The embroidery was often trimmed; the laces were of modest cotton or crocheted. The *porte-enfant* was a simple cushion covered with the family's best pillow case. After the ceremony, the guests gathered together over a home-made cake and a good glass of wine.

**30.** A child's first ceremonial dress is his or her Baptism gown. Since it is expected to do honor to the family as well as to the occasion, it is designed and prepared with great care. *Illustrierte Frauen Zeitung,* 1898.

**31.32.33.** A *porte-enfant,* a frilly baby's cap and a fabulous silk-embroidered satin christening dress which was used from the end of the 18th century right up until the 1950s.

24

**31.**

**32.**

**33.**

In those times, the two sacraments - First Communion and Confirmation - were received at around the age of twelve. The "Eton" and "Lord Fauntleroy" styles were the most preferred. The latter had been updated so that the jacket was now more open in the front and fastened with silk braiding. An enormous white collar with gathered flounce completed the effect. The sailor suit was also in vogue and the fabrics used for these special occasions were silk, linen or white velvet.

The girls were prepared for these sacraments in a religious retreat that could last up to a month. When they emerged, they were arrayed in white lace and embroidery, with veils, frilly caps, lisle gloves and carried embroidered almoners. The dress was, of course, long, and the flowing veil added to the image of a miniature bride. In the midst of the solemn hymns, the white roses and

heady perfumed incense, these young things resembled nothing so much as white spring flowers, those symbols of purity immortalized by Proust as well as by Garçia Lorca, who compared them to the flight of doves.

Pius X had laid down the rules for the ceremonies. But apart from the church liturgy there was another side to the occasion which took on more and more importance as time went on - the "pagan" side if you will, in celebration of these little kings and queens for a day. In recent years, the sacrament has regrettably become little more than a pretext for the ostentation of whatever meagre social prestige and economic well being one's family can boast of. And so, what should have been reserved a special status has become but another party the kids get dressed up for. Rustling silk taffeta dresses for the well-heeled little

26

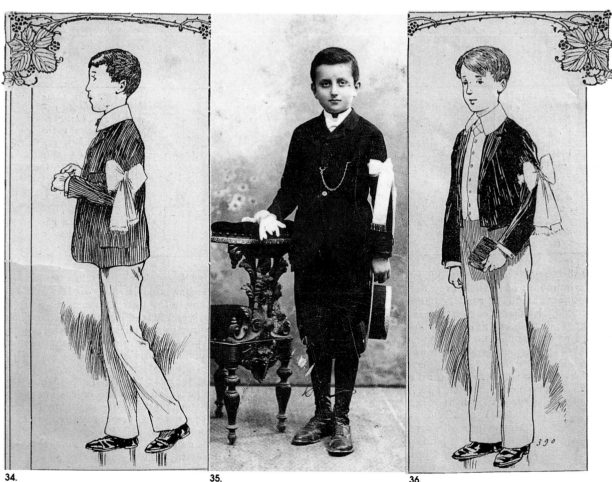

34.                                35.                                36.

girls or more modest fabrics for the not-so-rich go towards making this day in any case different from the rest, a day on which the most humble child can feel himself a little prince.

**34.35.36.** Three boys at their First Communion. Their trousers are either long or down to the calf. Their long socks, gloves and arm hand are, of course, indispensable-and white. The "Eton" jacket is made of black cloth while the trousers and waistcoat are also in white.

**37.** Pablo Picasso. *Comunion*, 1896.

**38.** For Protestant children, Confirmation is the most important religious ceremony. For the occasion, they may even dress in black. Catholics, however, carry out but simple variations on the First Communion theme. *Corriere delle Signore*, March 14, 1903. *Illustrierte Frauen Zeitung*, 1890.

37.

38.

## MEANWHILE, THE AMERICANS...

It took Americans a long time to come around to these ephemeral fashion concerns but when their "Buster Brown" look for boys comes on the scene it makes a splash. Buster Brown was a cartoon character created by Richard Foutcault and his style became an immediate success on both sides of the Atlantic, although as usual the English couldn't help looking somewhat askance at anything coming out of this land of rough and ready pioneers. Indeed, the outfit didn't really have a lot to do with what they were used to considering classic ceremonial dress.

It was a sporty suit with trousers gently tapering down to the knee. The jacket was double-breasted and hip length. The round, white collar was attached to the shirt with a stud button, as indeed all collars of the times were. A loosely made bow tie along with a straw hat (along Milanese-style lines) worn on top of short hair with a fringe completed the picture - except for the short boots. These were also specially named "Buster Browns" and were advertised as "correcting one's step at the same time as lending it style". The total effect was a great hit.

The girls were also starting to free themselves from mother's apron strings at about this time. Rising skirt lengths made getting on and off trams and horses a good deal easier and the new puffy-legged trousers held with elastic just below the knee like the old knickerbockers were just the thing for bike riding.

Not that the high-flying flag of elegant children's fashion ceased to wave - but for the first time it had some rather stiff competition. In short, the evolution of children's wear was moving along two distinct but parallel tracks: day-to-day dress and their still-splendid party dress.

A noted society woman at the beginning of this century, Donna Franca Florio, threw a party for her two children at their Sicilian Villa, Olivuzza. Her seven year old first born, Giovanuzza, was decked out in a white satin dress that came from the famous London store "Liberty". Darling "Baby Boy", her little two year old brother, was undoubtedly still dressed in long skirts.

Out of "Liberty" came another testimony to the elegance of these times: a floor-length dress in green silky satin with peach blossom embroidery. The style was a revival of the "empire" look: high-waisted, balloon-sleeved, with three skirt flounces. Accessories: a broad-brimmed straw hat

39.

and nose-gay. Other dresses of the time came from Italian lingerie makers. They were made of fine white cambric trimmed in Valenciennes lace and in *entre-deux* of Sangallo lace, were short, cool and eminently suited to those delightfully fresh, young things of the *belle époque*.

## THE WELL-STARCHED STATUS SYMBOL

In these years of transition, it is not surprising to find a mixture of the old and new. In spite of everything, reverent bows were still an important part of the educated families' children's repertoire.

Camilla Ravera used to spend her summer holidays at the royal estate of Valdieri as a guest of her uncle - superintendent of the Savoia family's holdings. As she recalls, "When members of the royal family arrived, life became a series of "do this" and "don't do that's". When we had to meet the always gracious Queen Elena, my brothers came to attention and we girls dropped into curtsies, just as we'd been taught".

It is no less of a surprise that starch becomes the status symbol of the age. Everything white, if it belonged to the privileged world of the upper classes or even if it were only meant to imitate it, gets starched. Not just the boys' collars but also the blouses, petticoats, dresses, hats and caps. Everything. Well-starched and at attention these children pose alone or wedged between the other members of the family with mummy in the middle to have their pictures taken. With eyes scorched and blinking from the magnesium lights they stand, living models of the heights of fashion. These photos, at the start simple daguerreotypes, came to take over the task that portraits had had in handing down to posterity evidence of the history of

29

40.

**39.40.** Party dress in the first few years of the twentieth century was often made of velvet and had large lace or linen cambric collars, at times embroidered. The knee-length cassock top covered the short breeches almost completely and had a belt woven through wide loops.

41.

children's fashions - a history that continues its course, winding down through the years between tulle, furbelows, lace and the insinuating odor of lavander...

During these first years of the 1900s, the photographer leaves his studio to immortalize the street fashions of the times, his shiny, brass and mahogany magic box and black cloth in tow. There, he turns his lens on little dark wool coats with winged matching hats, trimmed in precious chinchilla fur - the latest thing for the rich Milanese's little girl's muff.

Onto this cozy scene come the fashion magazines, raising a bit of a whirlwind. Their aim is to bring a little fresh air into this closed, stuffy milieu, to widen the horizons of the world of "woman's work" and fashion tastes. The new code strikes a net division between everyday wear and that meant for special occasions - those fetés to remember. Fot these, empire-waisted, short-sleeved, long dresses make a comeback. They are made of chiffon velvet and trimmed with swan feathers, as the cover of a 1913 issue of *Journal des dames et des modes* testifies.

**42.**

**41.42.43.** For those important occasions, the hats and caps of well-to-do children were adorned with ostrich feathers, ribbons and furbelows. *Regina*. 1905.

**43.**

## MOURNING DRESS

The children of those families who would leave them a coat of arms as well as a handsome cash legacy were usually included in the mourning rites for a close relative who had passed on. Should the deceased be a parent or grandparent, suitable clothing had to be worn. The dress code for the children was happily less severe than for the adults on these occasions. The girls were to be dressed in white or pearl grey with a black ribbon in their hair and a four-to-six inch wide, black arm band to be worn on the upper left sleeve of a dark overcoat for a full year after a parent's death, or for six months after a grandparent's passing on. The boys wore black or grey wool clothes and the sons away at boarding school (all those of the upper classes as well as those whose parents were trying hard to have them admitted to those classes) came home to take part in the funeral rites garbed in their school uniforms. Usually these were dark blue with a double row of gold buttons running down the front of the "spencers". In sign of mourning, these radiant buttons were covered over in black

tulle, as Francesco Caravita (in his own words, a "useless Neapolitan gentleman") reminds us. It was with his buttons so disguised that he plodded along alone behind his grandfather's hearse. The males too wore their arm bands for a year after the death. Moreover, for a full six months, riotous play, too-cheerful gatherings and anything that could possibly be interpreted as a sign of disrespectful distraction from suitably sad meditations were absolutely forbidden.

## FUTURIST GIRLS: THE STORY OF LUCE AND BARBARA

A dash of defiance was not totally disdained however - a tendency stemming from the Futurists, who had something to say about fashion as well, given that theirs was to have been a revolution on a world-wide scale. According to these prophets, clothes should be a mixture of the aggressive and the joyous, never hampering movement, bright and always different.

Giacomo Balla designed and produced a

32

44.

45.

**44.** That elegant look of well-to-do girls. *Fémina*, February 1, 1912.

**45.** Barbara Hutton in one of the official photographs of this child-millionaire taken in the 1910s. *Oggi*, December 1, 1949.

**46.** During the first World War, girls' fashions became a lot simpler, while the boys still sported their sailor suits. But even the girls wear hats or caps when it's time to go out. *La Moda Illustrata dei Bambini*, June 15, 1917.

dress for his daugheter, Luce (whose name is itself a manifesto), which was simple, indeed a bare essential in this lines, and brightened up with touches of white, turquoise and black. This short, round-necked dress with long, tight sleeves could easily pass as some famous designer's creation for today's modern evening wear.

Simplicity becomes in itself provocative. America's future legend, Barbara Hutton, was heir to the multi-million dollar Woolworth fortune at the age of four. For the official photographs, she was dressed in a free and easy, knee-length, short-sleeved, white dress with white shoes and knee socks and a droopy-brimmed hat encircled with tiny flowers. But the children of millionaires and intellectual futurists are not the only ones making news. The growing number of fashion magazines, besides illustrating

*toilettes* for the ladies, begin to provide picture cards for the kids and to offer advice on hygiene. And they are among the first to praise the benefits of sea water bathing - one of the twentieth century's greatest discoveries.

Magazines such as *Fémina* and *La Mode Illustrée* (which compete with *La Gazette du bon ton* and *Le Journal des dames et des modes* for a share of the market in France), along with *L'Eleganza, Il Corriere delle Signore* and *Margherita* help to spread the latest fashions of old and young alike. The kids have their own *Corriere dei Piccoli* from 1909 on, as well as the novels of Jules Verne, the exciting Salgarian adventures of Indian princes and that well-known, very Italian novel *Cuore*, which is then just going into its four-hundreth edition.

In a rare photo of young girls of the right

34

47.

48.

families, Biki, the future Italian fashion queen, Elvira Leonardi, poses at the age of two next to her grand-dad, the great Giacomo Puccini. She is wearing a lovely, fresh, short white linen dress with elbow-length sleeves. A sailor hat is on her head. The background for the snapshot is Viareggio, which, together with the Lido di Camaiore, was the popular holiday place among the in-crowd - from Puccini to D'Annunzio, from the divine Duse to Isadora Duncan. As Biki recalls: "We had a bathing hut on the stretch of beach known as "The Whale". On the beach I wore a red and blue striped wool costume. Once it got wet, though, it got rinsed immediately and I had to put on cotton rompers. Then there were my good clothes - like the dress I am wearing in the picture with grand-dad. Mother also had me put it on whenever we were invited to tea by Ms. Duncan while she was a guest of Ms. Duse at her villa in Lido di Camaiore".

**47.** A little boy in the 1910s in a white sailor suit with knee-length trousers buttoned jumper-style at the top. G. Barbier. *Costumes Parisiens*, 1913.

**48.** For special occasions a little girl during these same years wears a long velvet-chiffon dress trimmed at the neck, the sleeves and the hemline with luxurious white swan. *Costumes Parisiens*, 1913.

**49.** An outfit for six-to eight-year-old girls with plenty of frills, ribbons and frou-frou, even on the hat. The short white socks and white shoes complete this ultra-stylish summer look. *Costumes Parisiens*, 1913.

**50.** At the start of World War I, little girls' dresses hem-lines go way up. *Costumes Parisiens*, 1914.

49.

50.

## CHILDREN SOLDIERS

Two shots at Sarajevo announce the outbreak of World War I. The drawing room rites become more sober and fashions follow suit. In the first year of the war, 1914, Prince Humbert of Savoia's sailor suit gets longer trousers and the whole outfit turns dark blue. The large collar is edged in white, with a thin cord that cuts across the chest.

And then even the youngest Savoia children begin to dress up like soldiers, as does the Crown Prince when he accompanies his father Vittorio Emanuele III to the front or its vicinity. A documentary of the times shows him dressed in the same grey-green cloth of the soldiers' uniforms, with puttees on his legs and a short military cape draped around his shoulders. The descendants of Europe's other royal houses - the czarevitch son of Nicholas II of Russia and the grandchildren of Franz Josef, the Austro-Hungarian Emperor - do likewise.

36

**51.52.** The children of royalty are often seen in military dress. Here Czarevitch Alexis dons the uniform and decorations of a Husser officer while the Crown Prince of Japan, Akahit, is dressed as a naval officer of the 1905 war with Russia.

51.

52.

With material being rationed, girls' hem-lines go up nearly to what will be dubbed the "mini" in the '60s. But these are years of hardship and great suffering when these is no time or inclination to be scandalized - or fussy. Girls' dresses are short and long-waisted with a flounce or two beneath and that's all. A pair of long, thick, wool stockings cover these poor exposed limbs. And while the eagles fall, along with the Russian, German and Austro-Hungarian Empires, the little girls wore a little silk bow perched on top of their heads, perhaps in sign of joyful times that they hoped would someday return.

**53.** When compared to the party dress of Europe's youngsters, that of their American counterparts always looked a bit shabby. Soft, flowing fabrics and lines were the thing. *Pictorial Review*, October, 1919.

**54.55.56.** The Parisian *haute couture* dressmakers took care of both mother and daughter. For her creations, Jeanne Lanvin adopted flouncy taffetas and embroidered silk velvets. A silk ribbon wound around the waist and tied in a bow made a pretty belt for her demoiselles. *Les Modes*, 1917.

54.

55.

56.

# CHILDREN'S FASHIONS IN THOSE ROARING '20s

57.

## FASHION: THE TALK OF THE TOWN

The end of the war sees many changes in manners, customs and social etiquette. A new middle class arises - the so-called captains of industry who had succeeded in making their fortunes during the war and who, in Italy, are openly dubbed "sharks". These are the first years of the new influence from overseas, of jazz and of the "café society" that throws its drawing-room doors open to the new entrepreneurs, the intellectuals, the artists of the moment, and the new social climbers - all part of this new ambitious, cosmopolitan world labelled *Art Déco*. And these are the years in which a young American, Condé Nast, buys up a magazine on the brink of bankruptcy: *Vogue*. To it he adds some years later both *Vanity Fair* and *House and Garden*. With

Condé Nast, for the first time in the history of fashion publications, the most famous writers, from Cocteau to Gide and Virginia Woolf, along with the big-name photographers and the most ingenious designers are hosted in fashion mags - along with the best and newest fashions of course.

Nast's splendid penthouse apartment in Fifth Avenue becomes a gathering place of a coterie representing the latest in good taste. It is the scene of legendary parties hosted by him and his daughter, Leslie, dressed as though she had just stepped out of one of the glossy pictures in daddy's magazines. *Vogue* was to publish several international editions as well as a special edition dedicated to children's fashions.

In the magazines of those times, the net division between everyday wear for school or home and party dress remains in force. The sailor suit is the lone survivor of times gone by. As Susanna Agnelli recalls, it came in "....blue in winter, blue and white in spring or autumn and all white in summer.". The suit becomes a way of dressing and now has a matching blue wool coat with gold buttons and a large collar edged in white with anchors in the corners.

But that was a picture of a certain conservative austerity of English-sailor origin as practiced by the Agnellis. One phrase alone, written by the novelist F. Scott Fitzgerald in his short story "Winter Dreams", captures a quite different social frenzy which had infected old and young like in this new Renaissance. The eleven-year-old millionaire of his tale is described as being: "A china doll dressed in gold".

The fur coat is once again as popular as back in the Belle Epoque. Now, however, mothers (perhaps to ease a slightly guilty conscience?) take to trimming their little girls' coats and accessories with fur as well. At first, these take the form of big and small collars of mongolia or rabbit fur, of muffs and small round or oval shaped toques perched on top of shoulder-length curls. Then the collars begin to take on the strangest shapes and turn into proper stoles

58.

**57.58.** Evening dress for two young girls in marocain crêpe, antique gold, with lozenge motif in blue linen ribbon and again in lilac colored satin with ecru lace. Their escort wears the classic sailor suit in blue and white serge. *Gazette du bon ton*, Avril 1920. *La Moda illustrata dei bambini*, May 19, 1925.

59.

with little fur tails hanging from both these and the muffs. Clearly, such get up was not for going to school in. Rather, it was meant for special occasions like going to visit relatives with mother, who thus showed off both herself and her child to the best advantage. Finally, towards the mid '20s, the girls start to get full-length furs that are worn rarely and treated with great care, so that it would last and could be handed down to little sister. In any case, the girls are bundled up in nutria (the very rich ones!) or in ginger cat (the ASPCA hadn't set up business yet) or in rabbit. Colors ranged from white to brown, through all the intervening shades of beige.

**59.** Little girls' coats with fur trimming-*trés chic. Alla Città di Mosca*, 1926-1927.

**60.** To the already full stock of trimmings-collars, cape-like collars, cuffs etc. - of the children *à la page*, little fur coats with cloche hats or fitted velvet caps were now added.

## INVENTIONS AND DEVELOPMENTS

The history of fashion in the '20s must take into account the increasing concern with fabrics and technologies. The textile industry carries on the search, which began in the nineteenth century, for new man made fibers. Some of the fabrics that were presented at the *Esposition des Art Décoratifs* in Paris in 1925 caused quite a stir. They were more softly flowing than ever before, to allow free body movement. Rayon and jersey appear on the scene contemporaneously. These are indeed the "roaring" years. If "good manners" had been the pass word at the beginning of the century, what counts now is being at all costs "chic" - in one's way of acting, of speaking and, naturally, of dressing. The thing is to be fashionable and fashion becomes a whirlwind that is continuously making use of whatever the new technologies come up with - as fast as they can come up with it. A new ethos of "appearances" is in the making and the fashion revolution, especially as regards party dress, would appear to have reached its apex.

Gone are the corsets, the stiff bodices and petticoats, the black stockings and laced up boots. "In" now are bare legs, short lisle socks, and low-heeled shoes with delicate

60.

little side-straps. Little girls' dresses are knee-length with balloon sleeves, yokes of organdy pleats and perhaps pansies embroidered along the edges. Among the most popular fabrics for spring or summer is taffeta from which beautiful skirts, puffed sleeves and yokes with flower motifs are made. A collar, often of white muslin with matching motif, completes the effect.

These same styles are made up in velvet for the winter. The most-used color is sapphire blue. Next comes garnet red or bottle green. Onto them are sewn heavy lace collars and cuffs: macramé or Cantù lace or else heavy linen with open-work embroidery.

**61.** In the 20's little girls' elegant dresses are very short, they have a low waist or a loose style. *Gazette du Bon Ton*, 1922.

The creations of Sangallo and those *broderie anglaise* models for women by Coco Chanel also have much success. The girls wear shepherdess hats in Florentine straw decorated with cherries, ribbons and wild flowers - except when the party takes place at home. Then they sport a lovely big bow in their hair instead - a fashion begun during the war and continued ever since. Again Susanna Agnelli offers us a description of the way she and her sisters, along with brother Gianni, were decked out for a dinner with Prince Humbert of Savoia: "The four of us were dressed in rose-embroidered organdi, while Gianni had his sailor suit on".

As an alternative to this old-time favorite, the boys wore short pants in blue, brown or

42

**61.**

black velvet, a silk shirt, either with a flouncy collar or lace-edged, and a short waist-length jacket, fastened at the collar and open in front. Everyone wears short hair with a side-parting and flat-heeled shoes. A comfortable, soft, "babyish" look triumphs. Indeed, it is not too much to say that we finally have children dressed like children.

## A CHILD'S GARDEN OF DELIGHTS

The tailors and dressmakers are at work full-steam, though it must be admitted that the middle class begins to buy its clothes at the large department stores, particularly their children's everyday wear. But the seamstresses still have the task of copying those patterns appearing in the pages of the fashion mags devoted to elegant children's fashions.

France is still the unrivalled queen of the female fashion world. Along with the big names like Patou, Madeleine Vionnet and Coco Chanel, there also ranks a certain Jeanne Lanvin who, as the *Gazette du Bon Ton* notes, dedicates "a great deal of attention and feeling to her elegant creations

**62.** The sailor suit is not the only look for stylish little boys, *Fémina*, May, 1921.

**63.64.** Birthday party dresses. *La Moda Illustrata dei Bambini*, April 15, 1925. *Fémina*, March, 1923.

**65.66.** Still more suggestions for those special occasions. *Fémina*, May, 1921. *La Moda Illustrata dei Bambini*, April 15, 1925.

for young girls". There is a new need for taking great care in choosing fabrics, but also in cutting and styling: there are no longer elaborate decorations and trimmings to hide any eventual defects. It is during these years that the zipper also makes its appearance on the fashion scene.

There is little doubt that the styles of the '20s are still inspired by a timeless longing for the forbidden fruit. And there is not a shadow of a doubt that contemporary children's fashions have created a land of idleness and luxury in which there is a bit of everything for everyone: from hand-knit wool pullover dresses to socks and other accessories. Virginia Woolf, in *To the Lighthouse*, speaks of the children garbed in grandmother's lovely hand-knit wool dresses finished in an open-work embroidery that makes them appear dressed in lace.

Little girls can also be seen in three-piece suits composed of short jacket, bolero and flared skirt made of Lenci wool - a fabric so soft that just to touch it is a genuine pleasure. It so happens that the grown-ups have no difficulties in imitating them, and neither do the kids have any qualms in taking over the styles of their elders - for example their grey, flannel trousers and their three-buttoned jacket, worn by the youngsters for First Communions. This time, however, we are talking about real choices.

A certain new-found taste for the luxurious is in the air. The daughter of the noted Roman tailor Montorsi, Adriana, recalls: "My father used to take us to the race track at Capannelle in a Lancia convertible. It was a fashionable place, as were all the European high-society racing meets. In winter, I would wear a red frock coat with nutria-trimmed collar and cuffs and a cloche hat on my head.". For summer party dress, the latest thing was white piqué.

There is an admirable 1929 photograph of the Dashwood family taken by Cecil

67.

**67.** Being elegant is just as important in summer as in winter. Light-weight fabric such as these cotton muslin flowered prints are just the thing for pretty, feather-light dresses. *Jardin des modes*, March 15, 1929.

**68.** For receiving the sacraments, the girls are always dressed in white - earning themselves the analogy F. Garçia Lorca draws between them and the flight of timorous doves. The style, of course, changes with the fashion. In the '20s skirts were shorter and the veil cascaded from fitted caps while the boys wore knee-length trousers. *La Moda Illustrata dei Bambini*, April 15, 1925.

Tosca

Beaton in front of their house in the English countryside in which their oldest daughter is wearing an elegant, full-length afternoon dress in a pastel shade, with rounded collar, short, puffed sleeves and a sash at the waist - almost a variation of the turn-of-the-century theme. Her four-year old brother is wearing long overalls with a soft-collared, white shirt and a tie. Still considered working clothes by most, overalls thus begin their history as highly fashionable wear, being made out of typically fine material like velvet. The youngest member of the family, about a year old, looks particularly at his ease in his little white rompers.

**69.** The Dashwood family in the 1929 photo by Cecil Beaton.

46

69.

# POLISHED REFLECTIONS BY DESIGN
## THE THIRTIES

## MOVIE STYLES

The "Eton" and "Little Lord Fauntleroy" styles have long departed, as has the regrettable habit of putting boy toddlers in skirts. After the similar (in all but color - pinks, of course, are a must for the girls as blues are for the boys) fashions of the first few months of life, styles for the two sexes begin now to differ radically. The boys' rompers and girls' little dress with yoke are sure indicators of a changed way of thinking. It is coincident that during these years Montessori lays down her well-known principles and methods of education and from Vienna Freud reaffirms the role of psychoanalysis in discovering the individuality of the child, at the same time reiterating the child's overwhelming need for free expression - and that meant in his or her way of dress in both the private and public spheres as well.

The '30s then fly the banner of deliberate, polished style almost as if fashion had

**70.** The child star, Shirley Temple, in a gauzy, polka-dot, organdy dress, relaxes on the set. *Elle*, no. 2064, July 29, 1985.

already set out its vital designs and held up a collective mirror to make the final fitting an unqualified success. But that does not mean there were no longer any surprises.

For children these are curious times, contradictory from many points of view, even disturbing. The silver screen had recently been given a voice. Together, image and sound join forces in dictating fashion. These are the years in which Shirley Temple reigns over the fashions for the young. All over the world, girls will be trying to imitate her fair, shoulder-length, bouncy ringlets and her adorable little dimpled smile. Her hems come down to the knee - all skirts are coming down at about this time. Her dresses have a yoke and sport polka-dots, little white collars and balloon, or in any case full, puffed sleeves. For dressing up, white gloves and little black patent leather shoes with straps and buckles are "in", a must. Her little colored frock coats have matching, velvet collars, cuffs and buttons - simply, perfectly and impeccably "English" in style. Shirley Temple is a dream incarnated, the animated celluloide symbol of a perfectly happy childhood - and an endless wardrobe.

The fact is hardly surprising when we consider what was behind America's sweetheart - the rapidly expanding American fashion industry. It is, after all, the kind of thing America is so very good at. A case in point is the quintuplet birth of the Dionne sisters in Canada at the beginning of the 1930s. The occasion was immediately exploited to the hilt and became a mere excuse for launching a massive advertising campaign for every imaginable baby product: from food to clothes to furnishings for the nursery.

## DESIGNERS JUST FOR KIDS

In Europe, and especially in Italy, the dressmakers are busy copying the styles arriving from overseas via the movies, French fashion-plates or the pens of the latest designers. Among these is René Gruau - a new but important name for the '30s. He is a designer for *Dea*, the Italian high fashion magazine whose pages are full of the latest news on society and dress for the well-to-do woman. His sketches illustrate the most elegant styles of the times for both tiny tots and adolescents. For Christmas, 1934, he creates a yellow silk crêpe dress with yoke, sleeves, collar and cuffs, of one yellow and blue embroidered piece and has his little boys appearing in the family drawing room in short, black, velvet trousers, silk shirt and nut-colored "spencer" of *douvetine*.

All over Europe the most fashionable coat for winter is the Scottish plaid frock coat with fur collar, as worn by Lady Caroline and Lady Sarah Spencer Churchill; a two-button coat with a shawl-like fur collar down to the waist. With it are worn long stockings, white gloves and a velvet hat with turned up brim.

48

**71.** The famous Dionne quintuplets advertising the virtues of Palmolive soap.

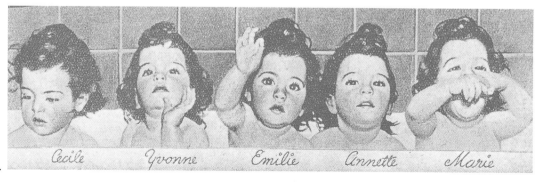

71.

Cécile    Yvonne    Emilie    Annette    Marie

## A POLITICAL STORM OVER CHILDREN'S FASHIONS

The most sought-after fabrics for their light, fresh quality are those in timeless organdy and linen, besides those in silk crêpe and *marocaine*. From "Liberty", cotton batiste prints are imported. At this time, England is still looked to for the last classic word in children's wear.

And it could have continued to be so for Italy as well, if the advent of Fascism had not

meant a search for a style that would disassociate itself completely from "Parisian perversions" and reflect the nationalistic tastes of the times. The regime's "Newspeak" attempted to wipe out the enemy's lexicon, even so far as fashion was concerned. Thus the "smock" becomes "nido d'ape" (honeycomb), the "redingote" (smock coat) is re-baptised "cappottino avvitato" (fitted coat) and the famous "Knickerbockers" are dubbed "alla zuava", in reference to the uniform worn by a corps of Algerian foot-soldiers created in 1831.

In Torino, in 1936, the Italian Fashion Board comes into being. In deference to the despotism of the regime, materials are dyed or printed in Romantren or Solidene. The Italian tailors and dressmakers pretend to sit

**72.** When the occasion is important, so are clothes, no matter how the time is spent! Style by Jeanne Lanvin, Rouff, Fairyland. *Femina*, August, 1933.

49

**72.**

up and take notice, but in reality everyone follows his own nose. The only real success the government will be able to boast will be having somehow forced the whole country into uniform.

A typical outfit for accompanying mother on one of her afternoon outings in the mid-thirties was a simple wool, red and green, plaid dress, low-waisted with pleats falling from the hip-length basque, a white piqué collar, probably well-starched, with a big bow fixed in front and a barret on top of either Shirley Temple-like curls or straight, side-parted hair falling to mid-neck length.

As usual, the special occasion called for the proper dress. As Adriana Montorsi recalls, "The dress we made for the five-year old daughter of the road contractor and cinema producer, Scalera, when she had a wedding to attend was of almond green wool, with slightly dipped waist-line, patch pockets we filled with sweets before delivery and the collar and cuffs in a shade of slightly darker green".

The most fashionable colors are greens of all shades, aquamarine blue, dusty rose and the color of parchment. But the state visit of the English royal family in 1936 sets off the rage for children's wear in white once more. At about this time, in the pages of *Dea* Gruau sketches a little girl's dress made of a series of white horizontal flounces which start from a yoke in some contrasting color and go down to the bottom of the dress, ending just under the knee. His little boys are in short trousers and a soft-collared shirt with a velvet spenser on top.

50

73.

74.

**73.** Back in the '30s, when he was only seven, Mickey Rooney played the role of a dwarf. *Elle*, No. 2064, July 29, 1935.

**74.** A child in the 1930s dressed up in the still-popular Little Lord Fauntleroy look. The suit is brown velvet and the shirt of natural silk.

**75.** In the '30s the habit of dressing the kids in white for special occasions, especially in the hot summer months, makes a come back. The fabrics used for these sheer, gauzy garments are piqué, linen, silk and cotton muslin. *Fémina*, September, 1930.

**76.** Flounces, plissé insertions and ribbon belts are all the rage for the girls' dancing lessons. Their partner is wearing an impeccable "Eton". *Dea*, October, 1938.

75.

## SUNDAY BEST

Although up to now we have been mostly speaking of the style of dress of privileged, upper class children, that was not to imply that the city's lower classes and even the working classes out in the country had no conception of what it meant to dress up for special occasions. The very name, "Sunday Best" was indicative of their awareness that there were certain days on which patched, everyday skirts and trousers would absolutely not do. Quite simply, the occasions for dressing up were Sunday Mass, a parish party or perhaps a family

76.

wedding. Here tradition called for the right touch of dignity and decorum in all details, including dress, which was simple and unpretentious and yet still a symbol of the seamstress-mother's aspirations to a better style of living for her child than what she had always known. And yet, whatever the item, it had to last long enough to be handed down to little sister as well as stay within a strict budget, and so there was no indulgence allowed, no frivolous frou-frou to go limp or delicate lace to perish.

Giovanni Pascoli immortalized his family's holiday best in tender-hearted verses, which, very freely translated, might go something like this:

Oh! Valentino looking once again,
Like a little bud of hawthorn!
All alone, to your faithful bramble,
you carry the soles of your feet,
wearing the shoes mummy made you,
the shoes you never more changed.
The shoes cost not a footstalk.
What cost was the suit she made you.
For her lovely prized money box,
tinkled and jingled no more.

It was a way of dressing that was rarely complete with all the accessories. As we can see, at least in the Pascolian years, the shoes were often missing, for the simple fact that the dress or suit itself had already consumed the family's meagre savings. Yet sometimes the suit was missing too. At the turn of the century and indeed into the '20s, the male members of peasant families "inherited" their fathers' wedding outfit, which, with a snip here, a tuck there and a hem that could be let down if need be, was made to serve for "special" occasions. The lapels, betraying the origin of the suit, were removed in preference for a more youthful "V"-neck look. The heavy cotton shirt had no collar. Years still had to pass before the lower classes got to imitate their "betters" in this style. The braces were buttoned to the inside of the waistband. When there were shoes, they were those with studded soles or even the kind having leather uppers and wooden soles that the Veneto farmers still call "sgalmare".

The girls' Sunday Best was likewise a hand-me-down from mother or big sister. In

77.

78.

those exceptional cases in which the dress is made from scratch, a dark blue woolette is used for winter wear. To this is added a home-made lace collar and a furbelow at the hem in an attempt to spruce up the otherwise modest creation. In summer the cost is usually more accessible. Thus, puffed-sleeve cotton dresses in checked or striped fabrics are made up, or perhaps they are multicolored flower prints on blue, pink or green backgrounds. Whatever the dress, it is always covered up with a full apron that protects it from household accidents and can be flicked off and out of sight when the expected callers ring the bell or when it's time to go out visiting.

An accessory that makes up for the simplicity of their dress are the little, gold hoop earrings that are put into the girls' pierced ears at an early age and usually stay with them to their wedding day. Another piece of "jewelry" commonly met with is the silver-plated ring with the Madonna's blue-enamelled image on it brought home as a present by some relative from his or her latest pilgrimage. The little gold necklace

traditionally given at First Communion completes the girls' jewelry collection. The boys, however, are even less fortunate. They have to wait until they are old enough to do their military service before they are allowed to possess even a watch. Of course, pictures of the kids in their holiday dress, with their teachers at the end of the school year in the class photo and in their First Communion dress are, as, ever, a must.

**77.** Twin outfits for brother and sister. The skirt on the girl's version is sewn to the top and has a fake buttoned effect, while the boy's shorts are genuinely attached by buttons at the waist. *La donna, la casa, il bambino*, March-April, 1933.

**78.79.** Sunday and holiday best: simple but elegant. *Grazia*, no. 125, 20 March, 1941; no. 128, April 10, 1941.

**80.** This little girl's Sunday Best is in blue woolette with white polka-dots. The little boy is in brown wool with trimming, collar and cuffs in beige silk or linen. *La donna, la casa, il bambino*, March-April, 1933.

53

**79.**

**80.**

## DUTY CALLS AND
## WE ALL FALL IN LINE

For Italian children nothing much changes until the late thirties when the government, playing its last cards of what will be known as the "Age of Consensus", decides to impose a regulation uniform on all kids from a certain age up. The results are veritable little soldiers in training for their warrior futures.

These uniforms are worn for the Saturday fascist rallies during the flag-raising ceremony, for parades and other official celebrations. Having to dress like everyone else meant coming down a few notches for the upper classes, who were used to dressing according to their wealth and status. The new dress code was hard - at least for the grown-ups. The kids obviously didn't give it much thought. For the lower classes, it might have even been a relief - an escape from the painful second-class quality of that Sunday Best described above.

81.

54

**81.** In the '30s the National Fascist Federation sent its Easter Greetings through the "son of the she-wolf" and his fascist salute.

**82.** The "Little Italian Women" in uniform celebrating the "Fascist Saturday" by rallying 'round the pennant'. *Lidel*, January, 1934.

82.

And so it was that from the age of five the boys wore the uniform of the "sons of the she-wolf" (Rome's of course) which was made up of grey-green, wool shorts, a black shirt and two white strips that come down and cross over the chest in a sash, fastened at the crossing point with a garish "M" for Mussolini. Finishing touches are a fez-like hat with bow, long, grey-green socks and heavy black shoes. At the age of eight, the wolves turned into "balillas", took off their white sashes and donned belts with cartridge-boxes and gaudy blue neck-scarves.

The girls are dubbed "the little Italian women" and are made to wear what almost seemed like mourning: a black, pleated skirt; a white blouse with either an "M" or the yellow and red symbol of the "Italian Youth Lictors" ("Gioventù Italiana del Littorio", shortened to GIL); a black-knit barret commonly called "the sock"; white stockings and black shoes. Over all was a black wool cape fastened with a chain and two studs at the neckline.

In this get-up the children went to their GIL national holiday celebrations. Christmas trees and Father Christmas having been banned, the fascist Epiphany, the local patron Saint's Day, the military victories and the official dates of the fascist revolution were all celebrated with great fanfare and a distinct air of xenomania in the Institutions for Motherhood and Infancy and the national recreational facilities, in praise of King, "Duce" and the sacred borders of the nation. Wooden and tin toys, celluloide dolls, candies, tangerines and sweet-meats were then handed all around...

## THE RICH AND THE PRIVILEGED

Those who want to show off their financial status and escape the strictures of Italian provincialism take off for foreign parts with the family. The fashion for learning foreign languages is not completely overwhelmed by the regime's nationalistic leanings and the children of the well-to-do continue to study French, considered the diplomatic tongue *par excellence* and German, for motives dictated by political alliance. English was disdained by the black-shirts and accessible to but few. And so they would pile onto the great floating hotel, the

**83.** The sailor suit is here to stay. This special First Communion version is slightly different from its predecessors in having the blouse tucked into the trousers and laced-up behind. *Le Petit Echo de la Mode*, March 20, 1932.

"Rex", with their sea-going trunks stuffed full of sailor suits for the boys and Ginger Rogers-style evening dresses of organdy and taffeta for the girls. These cruises were gay and carefree holidays from the troubled real world, the news of which, when it arrives at all, sinks in but slowly. Indeed, the sanctions decided against Italy for its neo-colonial politics in Africa have scarce effect, at least as far as fashion is concerned. The idea of saving money vanishes into thin air when rising hem-lines make frilly bloomers (made of the same material as the dress and edged in button-hole stitch and a touch of smocking) necessary. Fascist fashion dictates that the boys are no longer allowed to run about in long trousers "alla zuava" or to sport jacket lapels. A few manufacturers let themselves be persuaded to weave broom and a few families are convinced to save by making over the grownups' clothes for the little ones but these are isolated episodes that fall on deaf ears, much as Mussolini's 1938 speech in which he condemns what he saw as frivolous ceremonies requiring a certain fashionable way of dressing, decrying, among other things: "....high-class dress, taking tea at five o'clock, paying respects and holiday-making in the country....". The scarce attention being paid to the regime's wishes in the matter is

**84.** In Italy, May is the month of lilies and liturgical celebrations. These splendid Communion models are as up-to-date today, over fifty years later, as they were back in 1931 when they were designed. *Lidel*, May, 1931.

testified to by the periodical *Moda*, which, though it is still supposed to be the official publication of the National Fascist Federation of Garment Manufacturers, continues to print pictures and models of the latest elegant fashions, among them a little girl's sumptuous white frock coat with cap and buttons all in white velvet.

The will to live is still strong - and to live well. That's why the fascist demagogue's dictates are not obeyed. If anything, evening dress becomes even more elegant and daringly low-cut, and not just for the fully grown-up! Again, it is *Moda* that carries the

**85.** Some alternatives to the sailor suit for special occasions. The trousers are still long and come in white wool or silk, or perhaps are grey or striped - the "Eton" revisited - or even in black. The cut may undergo slight, original variations with time but the colors are still the classic grey, white, blue or black. *Dea*, April, 1937.

**86.** *Haute couture* for the English royal children. Elizabeth (before she became queen) and Princess Margaret in long, light, floating dresses, created especially by Jeanne Lanvin. *Fémina*, June, 1938.

story of how fabulously gay and sumptuous the 1939 New Year's Eve celebrations in Rome were, even with the Second World War under way and but a few brief months of "peace" remaining for Italy as well. It goes into all the details of how the young daughter of the Spanish Ambassador danced frenzied quadrilles all night, dressed in a skin-tight black bodice above a long skirt, ringed around in fascinating bands of deep - blue, violet, gold and silver and assures us that Roman high society compared not unfavorably. A final fling - or should we say a last goodbye to world destined to collapse under the weight of a conflict the extent of whose destruction was to leave millions of shocked and terror-struck human beings in its wake.

# THE YEARS
# OF HARDSHIP
# THE FORTIES

### AT FIRST NOTHING CHANGED

The outbreak of the war did not bring sudden changes to the world of fashion especially as regards children's wear. In June of 1940, when Italy entered the conflict, the man who was considered to be the best known fashion designer of the times, Mario Vigolo, thus laid down the law: "The lines have got to be essential and smart. The new fashions will be inspired by a sense of the casual, the sporting.". The social manners of the little ones remain pretty much the same as ever. In the drawing rooms, the bows and curtsies continue. The little boys have learned to kiss the ladies' hands and play *Le petit montagnard* for mother's guests. The little girls go on wearing classic, dusty rose dresses, a color that is still a favorite with mothers.

The girls' dresses almost invariably have a yoke that is pleated, ribbed or smocked. They come down to just below the knee and have frills at the neckline and wrists. One high fashion version of the style was created by a Roman dressmaker with a pansy motif on creme coloured wool (a miniature copy of a dress for mother) with short, puffed sleeves. The tiny tots wear much shorter dresses with the ever-popular honeycomb embroidery motif.

59

87.

Bows were a must for the hair. With time, rather than being made of crisped, silk taffeta, they are in rayon or shiny, artificial silk, flowing and with a frayed-look. The colours always matched that of the dress, usually shades of pink or blue, since red was definitely "out", white was deemed too "ceremonious" and black clearly connoted mourning.

In winter, when other forms of play were more difficult to organize, the children were accompanied to matinées where they are generally bored to tears - by both the plays thought to be "suitable" and the operas which decidedly were not. But their parents counted on their not being able to understand a word anyway, and besides, an appreciation of good music had to be encouraged in the young! For these excursions with mother or governess, the children wore their best clothes with frock coats or short, sack-like jackets over them and suede or fustian white gloves. Their shoes were either black or white and flat-heeled, with delicate straps of the kind done up on the side or, on a more *décolleté* style, the type that goes round the ankle and gets done up in front. For the head, the little velvet cap tied under the chin is still all the rage. In England, there is also an attempt by a certain Hardy Amies to bring back starched muslin petticoats that peak from underneath the hemlines - without success.

## NECESSARY COMPROMISES AND INDISPENSABLE EXPEDIENTS

In Italy as well as the other war-torn countries of Europe, during the winter of 1940-1941 certain changes begin to come about. The first ersatz furs in "pannofix", "laziofix" and "arnofix" appear. They are praised as being light-weight, elegant, lasting, and above all cheap; in reality, however, they were horribly thick and heavy. Such artificial stand-ins are also used that year for the children's coat collars and cuffs as well as for overcoats for the grown-ups. When these sold out, the manufacturers put "lanital" on the market. These are fabrics derived from waste cloth,

**88.** The British film actress Charlotte Rampling, a child in the '40s, is dressed in the wide-skirted organdy style popular at the time and wears a wreath of flowers in her hair. *Elle,* Semptember 23, 1985.

**88.**

**89.** The short smocked dress for tiny tots comes with matching short, puffed bloomers. *Jardin des modes*, March, 1930.

**90.** More and more, little girls' best dresses receive a smocked effect that is often further decorated with embroidered flowers or some other whimsical motif. *Jardin des modes*, July, 1949.

91.

**91.92.93.** The '40 mean hardship for most people all over the world, years when there is little time or need for dressing up. Indeed, for most, the important thing is having something to wear and what used to be considered decent for everyday wear becomes one's Sunday Best. *Bellezza*, January, 1942. *Mani di fata*, July 1, 1941.

from paper and milk. They are of poor quality, don't last and - as if that were not enough - are even rationed! In such a situation, compromise clearly becomes inevitable.

War-time afternoon wear is composed of long, wool trousers with a "formal" afternoon coat. Even a simple, synthetic blue crêpe skirt with numbers embroidered on the front, worn with an equally plain, white cotton blouse came to be thought of as elegant wear. In rebellion at this state of affairs, Tizzoni, one of the most fashionable dressmakers of the times, tore down the velvet curtains from his drawing room windows in order to make a party dress that could be considered suitable for the birthday of the daughter of one of his best clients. The result was a sumptuous short-sleeved dress with a full skirt and lace collar. The dressmakers, in short, do what they can to meet the demands of whatever remains of high society. Besides, one had to make a living somehow.

The Fontana sisters recall how: "One of our clients, a woman, brought us one of her lovely pre-war coats to be made over for her granddaughter. We turned out a lovely little frock coat with velvet collar and cuffs.". They remind us how fortunate those girls

92.

93.

**94.95.** Birthday celebrations for the young can be very important affairs. These girls (from left to right) are wearing velveteen dresses decorated in thin silk braid, in heavy grey crepe with red inlays and long puffed sleeves; a dress vaguely modelled on traditional peasant costume; and a wool knit that in Italy was no longer known as "jersey" softened with honeycomb embroidery for that smocked effect.

94. 95.

Berzeviczy Pallavicini

whose grandmothers still had their wedding trousseaus were. Their trunks chock full of muslin and linen night dresses which "....were just perfect for being recycled as First Communion and Confirmation dresses" were virtual treasure chests! To save on material, children's hemlines start inching up above the knee while, almost as some form of compensation, hair is worn long, to shoulder length. The most radical changes are in the boys' trousers' length. Never before have they been quite so short. Many old favourites are inevitably lost in the shuffle. At Eton, where uniforms are of course still worn, the traditional top hat is abolished because it would inhibit the use of the gas-mask, should it be needed. Even the flag comes in handy, though for what could hardly be considered patriotic purposes! As Margherita Milani recalls, "The winters were so terribly cold and those coats of ours so very light weight that the flag, which was made of wool muslin, made a great lining".

## A NEW LEAF IS TURNED OVER

When in 1945 this war which had left so much destruction in its wake finishes,

**96.97.** Sometimes the slightest touch can turn an everyday outfit into something quite special. Here it is a dazzling white shirt peeping out of this double-breasted, V-necked jacket and a perfectly knotted tie framed by an open cardigan that do the trick. *Fili,* February, 1941.

humanity turns to the task of reconstruction. Many things, however, have changed and will quite simply never be the same again. The world is obliged to turn over a completely new leaf.

Children's wear is at first imported from the U.S.A. - a nation among the "winners", but, more importantly, a country whose sacrifices and hardships had been almost solely economical, and thus a country left relatively intact and able to turn its attention immediately to the production of both necessities and frivolities. Its fashion industry is able to offer all the colour, the elegance and the appearance of well-being that a child's heart could desire. And so fashion, and along with it manners and customs, become once again the mirror and symbol of the changing face of society. In the elegant children's styles being produced in the post-war '40s, however, there is very little that can be called new. What we get is rather a strong echo of the familiar tastes and cravings of the past.

**98.99.** For his Confirmation, the German lad wears a singlebreasted, high-buttoned jacket in dark grey or blue wool. Little brother wears short trousers and a raw silk shirt. Another ceremonial dress. *Elegantissima,* 1949.

68

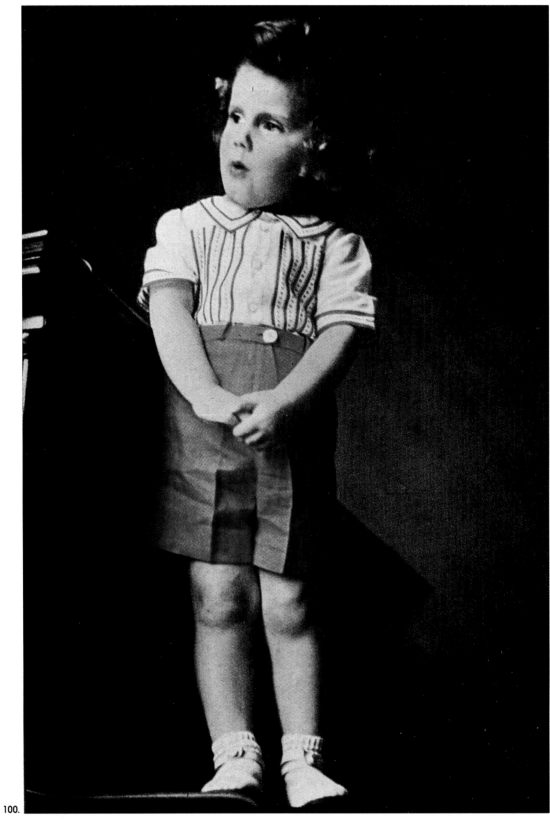

**100.**

**100.** A traditional look for the very young is a white silk or linen batiste shirt trimmed in the same color as the velvet or linen short trousers which usually come in red, emerald green, brown or sapphire blue. Photo by Porta. *Fili*, October, 1941.

# THE DECADES OF CONSPICUOUS CONSUMPTION THE FIFTIES AND SIXTIES

**101.** A photo of Faruk, the former King of Egypt, posing with his little boy, Fuad, who is dressed in classically elegant short trousers and embroidered shirt. The novelty consists of the tie which matches his trousers in fabric and color. *Oggi*, no. 275, July, 1957.

## FULL STEAM AHEAD - BUT STEP BY STEP

In the '50s and '60s, the fashion industry concentrates its efforts on satisfying a consumer fever that has left few untouched. At first, it is fed with simple, rather hurriedly put together, practical styles that toot the horns of equality and spontaneity. The dictates, in fact, are few.

Later on, however, with reconstruction well on its way and virtual economic booms taking place in Italy and elsewhere, attention turns from quantity to quality and children's fashion designers begin once again to offer their market the traditional choice between normal, everyday wear and Sunday Best for those speical occasions. Reviewing the situation of these years of well-being, Rolf Pasold, general manager of the important English manufacturer of children's clothes, "Ladybird", recalls: "New fabrics and new

technologies on the one hand and a higher standard of living on the other gave both designers and manufacturers unhoped for opportunities. Within very few years, children's wear went from being devoid of any direction to being the stimulus of a veritable fashion industry, where the accent fell not only on quality and wearability but above all concentrated on style".

**102.** Hollywood star of the '40s and '50s, Joan Crawford, poses here with her children for a snapshot that was destined to launch a new fashion. The bows in Christina, Cathy and Cindy's hair, that around the actress's neck and Christopher's tie are all made of the same silk fabric. *Oggi*, no. 12, March 22, 1951.

**103.** Valentina Cortese, the Italian stage actress, and Hollywood's Richard Basehart, pose here with their son dressed in the 1950's version of the ever-popular sailor suit. *Oggi*, no 27, July 5, 1950.

**104.** Even American kids have their Sunday Best, *Life*, May 4, 1953.

102.

103.

The high fashion dressmakers make a comeback and their hand-crafted, stylish creations for old and young alike are once more awarded due appreciation. But, as the saying goes, necessity is the mother of invention and myriad new needs and demands call forth a new and exciting inventiveness in these post-war years: from fire-resistent synthetics to the T-shirt, mix and match coordinates and that egalitarian item in elasticized denim, blue jeans, which were to become as inevitable as measles and were to add an ubiquitous touch of style - even to the first few months of most babys' lives. The fashions of the times were at least apparently intent on wiping out class divisions and bringing to the fore the uniqueness of childhood. Yet it did not take long before the need for something "more", something "special" made itself felt and before both large and small manufacturers took notice and aimed to please. If we may point to one overwhelming feature that distinguishes these years, it is clearly the fact that fashion is now running on several parallel tracks simultaneously. *Haute couture* may still hover there at the top of the pyramid, but the levels below are certainly

72

**105.106.** Though slightly less ceremonial, the bow tie is a popular option to the long one for formal occasions. *Bimbi Moda*, no. 27, 1957.

**107.** American-style short trousers buttoned to a white embroidered shirt. The oufit is made of "Terital" - at that time the latest no-iron, spot-proof fabric on the market. *Mamma e Bimbi*, summer, 1961.

105.

107.

no less dynamic, given an industry capable of providing quality and style for all tastes and pocket-books. Joseph Sassoon put it perfectly when he noted that: "The desire for what was different as well as for flaunting one's social status had been given new, complex and quite sophisticated means of expression".

**108.109.** Even the big-name Italian designers like Veneziani, Mingolin, Guidi begin to dedicate their talents to kids of all ages. Here we have an elegant little frock coat by Veneziani and a party dress with frills and lace by Enzo. *Mamme e Bimbi*, no. 4, winter, 1951.

108.

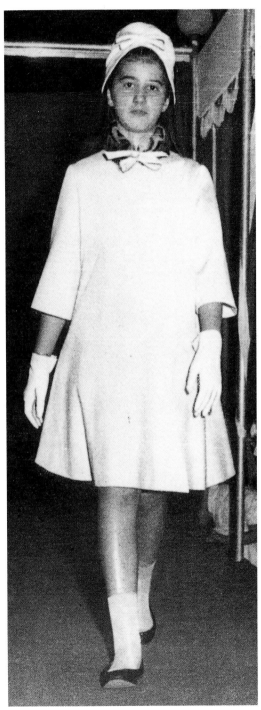

109.

occasion. The three-and five-year-old boys are in their grey short trousers, white shirts and blue cardigans. This habit of making all your kids wear the same thing is a long-standing tradition among the best families, but is obviously something the kids themselves often resent, and fiercely. Little one and a half year old Serena is dressed in a

111. In the '50s, there's a strong fashion wind blowing from the States. As so many of his contemporaries, this little boy is dressed in an American-style white, collarless jacket and blue shorts with a dark bow tie, *Mamme e Bimbi*, no. 2, 1961.

110.

**110.** A dress in the new synthetic "Delfion" with a pleated yoke and a full skirt kept crisp with a stiff petticoat. A wreath of flowers in the hair and classic black patent leather little girl's shoes complete the festive look. *Bimbi Moda*, no. 25, 1957.

## NOTHING *TOO* HEADY, PLEASE

The period that follows is characterized by a refined elegance in children's party dress. It is a dreamy, slow-moving time that dares not to dare too much. On New Year's Eve of 1955, the children of one of the future protagonists of Italian politics, Giulio Andreotti, are getting dressed for the

**112.** Summer fashions in satinated cotton come in a host of prints, solids and stripes, like those of this boy's straight, collarless jacket. Design by Walter Albini. *Bimbi Moda*, no. 25, 1957.

112.

short, elegant white dress with round collar and long sleeves.

Christina Onassis, who is six that year, celebrates New Year's Eve on her millionaire father's yacht, the *Christina*, wearing a short, subtle-waisted, print dress with collar and cuffs. Her hair is parted into two pig-tails and tied with ribbons; her slightly older brother, Alexander, is in short trousers, shirt and cardigan, long socks and

**113.** Fashions for First Communion and Confirmation are still extremely formal and unbendingly traditional. They are made up in wool or velvet for the boys and silk or cotton muslin, organdy or silk crepe for the girls. *Marie Claire*, no. 12, March 21, 1953.

**114.** Without a doubt the dress worn here by Leopold III and Liliane de Rethy's older daughter for the presentation of her new baby sister to society is just the thing. *Epoca*, no. 315, October 14, 1956.

typically aristocratic English footwear, something like "Church" style shoes.

Things stay pretty much the same for several years. Everywhere grey, flannel, knee-length trousers with those two little buttons at the hem can be seen. On rare occasions, some adventurous parent may alter the fabric of the model to bright red, emerald green or simple black velvet and spruce up the shirts with frills or Peter Pan collars, to the envy of the children whose own folks have a horror of the "camp" and so stick to their conservative tastes. The little girls still wear gauzy, organdy, wool muslin or linen batiste dresses, smocked in rosebuds, garlands and butterflies. And so it goes, until Charles of the House of Bourbon, future king of Spain, poses for an official photograph in a classic blue blazer with a solid colour tie.

**114.**

115.

78

## THE *ENFANT PRODIGE*

In 1956, the fame of a verse-writing, eight year old French girl, Minou Drouet, spreads all over Europe. Her spontaneously dashed off verses reveal a maturity far beyond her years together with a pessimistic streak that, although uncommon in one so young, nonetheless fails to overwhelm a certain natural buoyancy:

> *Cacahuéte, cacahuète,*
> *Oh que la vie est bête.*

that it to say,

> *Peanuts, peanuts*
> *How silly life is!*

This little poetess becomes, if not quite a legend in her own time, then at least an undeniable cultural event that creates quite a stir in the drawing rooms of France and beyond. Her face appears on the covers of several of the popular magazines of the time and she gives some rather mischievous interviews that set tongues wagging. In short, Minou becomes a virtual *enfant prodige*, a model for young writers and, inevitably, an example of how to dress for her numerous, curious admirers.

When Minou appears in mother's drawing room to receive the press and the photographers, she is smartly but not ostentatiously attired. A snapshot taken of her at this time portrays a smiling little girl (according to the good manners so insisted upon in the homes of the middle classes in the fifties), seated at a piano (so she is musical as well!) and wearing a short, wide skirt, and flower-embroidered bib and a white batiste blouse with puffed sleeves and rounded collar. Her long curly locks are tied back in a pony tail.

A six - year - old Spanish boy also rises to fame at about this time because of the part he played in a popular film of the time, *Marcelino pan y vino*. Pablito Calvo is the little actor who has the audiences in tears over how badly he is treated and how sad and alone he is. He actually gets received by Cardinal Lecaro of Bologna and goes to the appointment dressed, as was expected, "to kill", in what were by then the classic, short grey trousers, a white shirt, adouble-breasted, square-cut jacket and a regimental, verticle-striped tie. His white knee socks and laced-up shoes completed his faultless attire.

**115.** Fresh, crisp cotton prints designed by Walter Albini that mirror the fashion tastes of these years. *Mamme e Bimbi,* summer, 1962.

**116.** Embroidered organdy for Sunday Best.

**117.** Tea time in velvet. Designs by Walter Albini, from *Mamme e Bimbi,* autumn, 1961; spring, 1962.

**117.**

# THOSE VERY SPECIAL
# OCCASIONS: SOCIETY WEDDINGS

The year 1949 is a whirl of high-society events that testify to a widespread desire to get back to good living. Among these is the wedding of Prince Fleming of Denmark to a girl with no royal blood in her veins, Ruth Nielsen. The Prince's love match means he has to give up the throne but the wedding is nonetheless conducted in royal style. The numerous bridesmaids are dressed in white organdy and their yokes are edged in frills.

**118.** With the end of the nineteenth-century, elegantly dressed children began to take part in society weddings as pages and bridesmaids. *Illustrierte Frauen Zeitung*, January, 1885.

**119.** A wedding in the world of high fashion: the bride of Jean Charles Worth - member of a long line of famous tailors - surrounded by her bridesmaids and two pages in black velvet. *Fémina*, June, 1921.

**120.** Maids of honor decked out in frills, ribbons and polka-dot embroidery. *Fémina*, February, 1924.

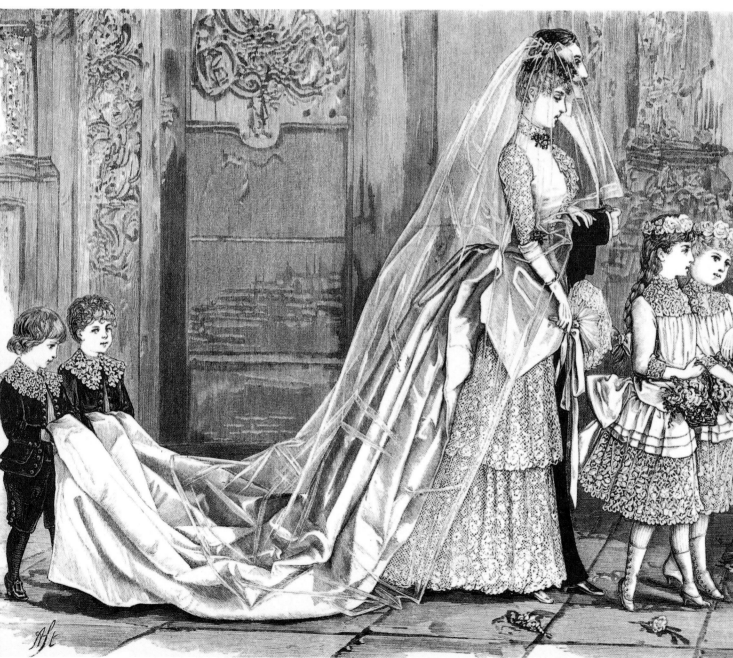

119.

On their heads they wear white caps the fronts of which are raised up to form diadems.

The wedding of Grace Kelly and Prince Ranier of Monaco in 1956 sets the world a-buzz. The nervous but radiant bride is flanked by two sets of bridesmaids. The adolescents wear long, yellow, organdy dresses with full-flared skirts kept aloft by equally full petticoats. Their gowns have long, full sleeves which are gathered at the wrist and matching yellow silk waistbands. On their heads are wide-brimmed white

120.

121.

hats. The little girls are in gauzy, organdy as well, this time white, decorated with the same flowers as they wear in their head wreaths. Their socks are short and white, as are their shoes and gloves. The pages are in eighteenth-century-style, pear-shaped short trousers, fastened at the knee. Having children in one's wedding party is a habit that became really fashionable in this century and was especially in vogue in the first post-war years. After all, little ones are supposed to bring good luck and are also a sort of allegory for the children the newlyweds may hope soon to have. And so they participate in all the best society weddings and pose for photos holding the bride's train, raising her lace or tulle veil, walking before her down the aisle with the wedding rings balanced on a velvet cushion, or perhaps merely accompanying her down the aisle and then following the newlyweds back up it after the ceremony has ended.

**122.**

**121.** Pink and white satin and ecrù lace for these two little train bearers at a society wedding in 1929.

**122.** Bride, bridesmaids and pages - all attired by Jean Patou. *Fémina* 1939.

**123.** Organdy, cotton and silk accompany the bride down the aisle. The gauzy, loose-fitting sleeves add a decidedly romantic touch to this pretty picture. *Fili*, no. 21, September, 1935.

**123.**

**124.**

**125.**

**124.** These bridesmaids are in white organdy with box pleats and embroidered blue fleur-de-lis by that magic fashion name of the '50s, Dior. *Plaisir de France*, 1949.

**126.**

The children are usually those of relatives or close friends. The cast may include a sole little girl or a "couple" in miniature or even a large, equal number of boys and girls for the most important nuptials. Consultations and preparations begin long before the established date. The cut, fabric, colour, decorations - so much has to be decided! There are the pages in silk and velvet to think about and then the bridesmaids in what are usually long silky gowns in soft pastels, or even in white along with the bride, with the touch of colour provided by their waistbands, the wreaths of flowers wound in their curls, by embroidery or perhaps by little flowers stitched here and there upon their full skirts. In summer, the boys are allowed to wear long white linen trousers. Their white silk shirts have full long sleeves that finish in tight wrists and they sport coloured cummerbunds. The girls are in pastel-colored linen or piqué. These exqusitely-dressed children usually

127.

85

**125.126.127.** More wedding costumes for boys and girls. At this point, what novelty there is lies mainly in the choice of color and fabric, the styles tending to follow what are considered by now the classic lines. *Jardin Des Modes*, 1940; *Fili*, March, 1940; *Fémina*, May, 1931.

125.

126.

128.

**128.129.130.** The little and bigger bridesmaids surrounding Grace Kelly at her wedding to Prince Ranieri of Monaco wear yellow and white. *Epoca*, April 29, 1950. Egon von Fürstenberg in velvet trousers and a "V"-necked, short-sleeved shirt of silk crepe for his sister's wedding. *Settimana Incom*, no, 40, 1955. This American bride chose broderie anglaise for her little bridesmaid and a *grenadier* uniform for her page. *Vogue*, May, 1952.

129.

130.

can be counted on to behave themselves as a result of constant reminders from all sides to be good and straight-faced and not to do this and please! not that! - at least until the end of the ceremony proper. Then they are happily allowed to run about, their cheeks flushed and mouths stuffed with cake and sweets.

And the custom still holds good today as we near the turn of the century, at least for the most important weddings, although it seems that the relaxed atmosphere of the latter 1980s has not failed to take liberties with the wedding attire in even the most traditionally conservative environments, as the latest English royal wedding of Andrew, Prince of York, and Sarah Fergusson can testify. The bride may be pretty and lively but she certainly cannot be said to have much of a pedigree. And then, the neckline of her gown was decidedly risqué, as were those of her bridesmaids. The pages, on the other hand, seemed to have walked straight out of Edwardian times in their elegant little sailor suits and straw hats.

**131.** A sweet little member of the royal wedding party of the Duke of York in 1986.

**132.** In the 1980s, it's not impossible for kids to find themselves at their own mum and dad's wedding! These girls have invented a new style of train bearing - dad's tails! *Moda in Baby*, no. 9, 1984.

131.

132.

# TIME OUT FOR FUN AND FANCY DRESS

## 'CARNIVAL-TIME': JESTS IN EARNEST

The origins of Carnival festivities are remote and shrouded in mystery. One thing we do know, however, is that in Roman times these celebrations coincided with the festival of Saturn and its unrestrained and unrivalled merry making and wild revelries. Its "modern" counterpart in Europe started in about 1600 and was inextricably linked to the once rigidly imposed Catholic rituals of fasting and abstinence that were to come during the forty days of Lent. In fact, even today "Carnival" time goes right up to Ash Wednesday, the day signalling the start of Lent. At Köln, the Catholic capital of Germany, *Fasching* is celebrated with the same rather weighty gaity and mirth of *Mardi Gras* in France or Rio de Janiero. Though it was instituted to commemorate the slaughter that Queen Esther succeeded in warding off, the Jewish holiday of *Purim*, celebrated in the month of *adar*, falling between February and March, is similar in its festivities. Carnival is the time for children to get dressed up in traditional costumes and indulge ravenously in the traditional Carnival sweet: flaky, light, pastries covered with vanilla-flavored confectioner's sugar.

**133.** P. Picasso: *Paul dressed as Harlequin*, oil on canvas; *Musée Picasso*, Paris.

**134.** A modernistic young lady in the beginning of the twentieth century dresses up - with wings. Her little sister, less futuristic in her taste, shows a penchant for ferns. *La Mode Illustrée*, 1909.

And so Carnival reaches its dizzy, dazzling climax in the week before Lent and the forty days of abstinence from meat and all dainty morsels begin. Venice soon became the self-appointed capital of fancy dress revelries whose utter sumptuousness and near-madness went unrivalled. Here behind masques, anonymous commoners danced and sang and jested, freely rubbing elbows with the nobles. Happily for us, this *merry making of old and young alike was captured on canvas by Pietro Longhi in the 1700s.*

For the aristocratic childen it was a time when the court tailors and dressmakers were busy creating fabulous costumes with masques to match in which they'd then tour the vicinity in carriages, "with great mirth, giving liberally to all the inhabitants of the country-seat", as the Medici children's tutor recounted. With the masqued children's ball that Queen Victoria and Prince Albert gave in 1859, a new custom of throwing these lavish parties started up in all the courts and aristocratic drawing rooms of Europe. The ball in Elizabethan dress given by the Marquise of Salisbury in the splendid family castle at Hatfield is described by the author of *Alice in Wonderland*, Lewis Carroll, in a letter to a friend of his: "...the children's fancy dress ball I went to yesterday was absolutely splendid. In that genuinely Elizabethan castle, all the children were dressed up in costumes of those times. The festivities began with a grand and sumptuous procession....". Naturally, as this and other memoirs of the times amply testify, these children's costumes were exactly the same as those for adults, only on a smaller scale.

**135.** The custom of celebrating "Carnival" by dressing up in what were often extravagant costumes began in about the seventeenth-century. In this late eighteenth-century print, among Pierrot and the various cavaliers and shepherdesses, we even have a dog in fancy dress! *Le Moniteur de la Mode*, December 27, 1879.

135.

**136.** The costumes proposed by *Fémina* in their February 1, 1912 issue include Tytil and Mytil, the characters from Maeterlinck's *The Bluebird*, and this Scotsman in taffeta kilt.

**137.138.** In 1900, the green toad, the bunny rabbit and the beetle parade side by side with the little marquis, the chrysanthemum and the rococo lady-in-waiting. *La Saison*, January 16, 1900.

**139.** The little elf is a French fashion suggestion for male tiny tots. *Costumes Parisiens*, 1914.

## FREE REIN TO THE IMAGINATION: THE TWENTIES

The vivacity and euphoric atmosphere of the '20s have their liberating effect on the celebration of Carnival time as well. Gone are the crinolin and powdered wigs, the fake beauty marks, the minuets, the bows and the curtsies. Victorian stuffiness and trappings are relegated to the attic and a new and inventive breath of fresh air sweeps the Carnival scene, invades its riotous parades and mounts upon its allegoric floats. Amidst confetti and streamers, France's Nice and Italy's Viareggio vye with each other for the coveted title of "Queen of Carnival".

Fashion magazines like *Dea* and *Le Journal des dames* suggest costumes based on children's fairy tales and nursery rhymes: the bat; lady bug; bunny rabbit and butterfly. Those imitating flowers are some of the most imaginative and creative. A few

bits of brightly colored fabric, an ounce of imagination and a few helpful hints from the magazine are all that's needed to transform a child into a dazzling poppy or gay sunflower. To create a sweet little lily of the valley, a simple white dress is sprinkled with artificial ones. Add to this a diadem-shaped garland for the little girl's hair and she's ready to parade down the avenue the Thursday before Lent (one of the main days of the celebrations) to everyone's delight and admiration.

Then, besides the costumes based on the heros and heroines of classic children's literature like Pinocchio, Peter Pan, Little Red Riding Hood and a host of multicolored pirates, the Italian Commedia dell'Arte's bag of tricks is rummaged and a long line of Columbines, Harlequins, Punchinellos and Pierrots (the smaller the child, the bigger his or her collar) is the result. The well-known characters of Manzoni's novel *I promessi*

94

**140.**

**141.**

*sposi* are also a source of inspiration and Italy's Catholic background gives rise to numerous angels with gold cardboard wings, perhaps even posing for a *tableau vivant* of the Annunciation. But these are the classics. The countless beauty products strewn upon the dressing table which in the '20s made its appearance in every woman's *boudoir* didn't fail to inspire some of the most creative costumes of the day. A simple, short white dress and a bag of swan feathers was enough to transform a little girl into a darling little powder puff - just like the one in mother's Art Deco powder box that Lalique designed for Coty.

In the '30s, the appearance of crêpe paper makes things even easier - and a lot cheaper! Mothers, grandmas and maiden aunts burn the midnight oil to produce the most exotic creations out of this new "material". In this era of widening social and cultural horizons, Carnival time resembles nothing so much as a trip "Around the World in Eighty Countries". The females are arrayed as little Dutch girls or even *Madame Butterfly*, while the boys are all mad to be Indian braves, though some are quite happy with a paper replica of the feathered Tyrolean hat.

**140.-143.** Towards the end of the '20s, traditional Carnival canons get put aside and the imagination is given free rein. Some of these modern creations include: the artist's palette; the bat; the powder puff and the record. Designes by Flora Gandolfi, from *Fancy Dress.*

142.

143.

**144.**

**144.** For a fancy dress ball thrown by Milanese high society in the late 1930s, these two sisters arrive in futuristic dress created by the theater costume house, Caramba, Photo by Baratelli, Milano.

**145.** For the same ball, another two sisters come dressed in 1870 fashions, once more designed by Caramba. This oil painting immortalizing the event is by Bernardino Palazzi. 1938. Photo by Betty Brunelli.

## THE ADVENT OF CARTOONS

The little heros of the comic strips and cartoons of the past had no influence on children's fashions. What happened was rather the opposite. For example, those two incorrigible pranksters of *Corriere dei Piccoli* (published in Italy since the first decade of the century), Bibì and Bibò, are dressed up like little upper-middle class kids starting with the latter years of the '20s. When playing their nasty tricks on surly Captain Cocoricò or their governess, Tordella, they are decked out in long, striped trousers and "spensers" or the ever-popular "Eton". Walt Disney had no doubts about how to dress his creation of the '30s, Donald Duck. The sailor suit was still the most popular boys' outfit. And so Donald has two of them in his wardrobe: his everyday blue one with the red bow and the black version for special occasions that he wears with a little bow tie. For over fifty years now these have served him well.

**146.147.** A home costume and birthday party all in one. The birthday girl is a little Dutch girl for the day in a crêpe paper costume, while one of her guests arrives proudly dressed up as a swaggering buccaneer in red velvet with shiny black patent leather boots. 1939.

**148.-150.** Famous cartoon characters of the '30s - in their Sunday best! The designs of Donald Duck are, of course, Walt Disney's: from *Il Giro del Mondo di Topolino & C.,* Mondadori, 1967.

146.

147.

148.

150.

149.

151.

**151.** An improvides, rustic Carnival of the 1980s, Pellissetti Archives. Venice.

**152.** In the '50s the in look for the adventurer and the hero was all-American. Here are your typical trigger-happy cowboys in their famous ten-gallon hats.

152.

153.

## THE SIGNS OF POP-CULTURE

World War II puts a stop to such frivolities for a few years, but as soon as it's over, Carnival comes back to take everyone's mind off unpleasant thoughts and memories as effectively as ever. Once again, the naturally perfect backdrop that Venice provides earns it the reputation of queen of the festivities. Every Italian city has its celebrations, however, which are now inevitably affected by the emerging symbols of the new consumer society. Modern technology now plays an important role

**153.** The Roman Carnival of 1951 owes its creations to the famous Zingone tailors and dressmakers, designers of children's wear since the turn of the century. Photo by the "Excelsior Service".

**154.-157.** The Turk, the swan, Napoleon and Disneyesque characters like the twin chipmunks, Chip and Dale, are now added to the traditional repertory of children's Carnival costumes; *Bimbi Moda*, N. 27, 1957.

**154.**          **155.**

**156.**          **157.**

**158.159.** In the '60s, costumes take on the flavor of the not too-distant past as well as of traditional popular and national dress. Walter Albini proposes a "Charleston" swinger, a "pasha" and a *Mademoiselle Empire. Bimbi Mode*, autumn, 1962. Another "Empire" look, this time with a pastoral touch, a chinaman and a bull-fighter are suggested as easy and not too expensive costumes by *Annabella*, no. 8, February 25, 1962.

158.

through television, which become the prompter of the new Carnival costumes: from astronauts to aliens from outer space-Mazinga, Superman, Spider Man and the like. The streets are invaded with apocalyptic monsters rapidly turned out by a new and booming industry for the waiting toy shops and department stores. And then there are the more singular products of this post-modern age: the walking record; the tin of peas; the gas tank - all ingeniously constructed with cardboard, foam rubber and coloured felt tip pens. What counts more than ever is the imagination and a new-found freedom of expression that takes the

159.

form of the simplest but well-aimed stroke of lipstick or dab of powder that succeeds in communicating at a glance any mood: from gaiety to sadness and the tearful melancholy of a *Pierrot Lunaire*. A far cry from the elaborate Elizabethan costumes once in vogue, this too is Carnival, though the odd lady-in-waiting in dusty rose furbelow and powdered wig can still be glimpsed braving the hordes of robots, along with a few black-caped and masqued Zorros and some haughty, plumed musketeer of yore. Uniforms too are still quite fascinating costumes for many kids - but only the

160.

extravagant operetta-type trappings reminiscent of a glorious, gallant past. Audrey Hepburn's little boy went to a fancy dress party in 1975 as a Hussar-only to find the idea had been considerably less original than they'd thought!

**160.161.** In the '70s, anything goes. Just give the kids some party hats, noise-makers, confetti and streamers, a bit of free rein and sit back and watch! Photo by Manfredi Bellatti and Richard Imrie, *Vogue Bambini.*

# THAT EXOTIC TOUCH

Of all present-day traditions that have been carefully preserved and handed down from generation to generation, the "festival of the dolls" held yearly in Japan is surely one of the most noteworthy. It involves all little girls of a certain social status up to the time they are six. On the day of *Hina maturi*, which takes place on the third day of the third month of the year, the little girls put on their elegant kimonos, adorn their hair with peach blossom and slip a pair of traditional sandles made of silk and brocade especially for the occasion on their feet. They are then ready to receive their guests and show them their specially arranged collection of dolls. These are not just any dolls but are precious collector's items and heirlooms dressed in precious reproductions of genuine imperial court dress and representing all the members of the ancient court beginning with the emperor and empress and including the ministers, the ladies-in-waiting, the nobles, the servant, musicians and family gods. A specially prepared saké with practically no alcohol content and colored rice sweets are served to the accompaniment of ancient songs and tunes in celebration of this holiday that is looked forward to with great anticipation all year long.

**162.** A singular carnival costume of the '80s: a bold little miss of the once-again fashionable bon ton plays the "bersagliere". Photo by Marco Lanza, *Moda in Baby*, no. 18, July-September, 1986.

**163.164.** *Hina maturi*, or the festival of the dolls, is not the only time little Japanese girls and boys get dressed up in their very best. During the week of *shogazzu*, three, five and seven year-olds get taken to the Shintoist temple to receive a special blessing. *Moda in Baby*, no. 9, April-June, 1984.

52. 163. 164.

# TOM THUMB TAKES GIANT'S STEPS: THE SEVENTIES AND ON TO THE YEAR 2000

## A DASH OF THE PROVOCATIVE

Children's fashions in the beginning of the '70s naturally feel the reverberations of that upheaval that had hit the adult world not long before. Protest and change are in the air together with a whiff of madness that can't help but invade the world of fashion as well, leaving its free and easy mark, no matter what the occasion.

Quite clearly, one side of the story is the low cost of these clothes, first among them being these jeans and mini skirts that from London's Carnaby Street quickly spread world-wide. The other, however, is a longing to shatter all the old molds of the bourgeois *bon ton*, to break out, be free, or, as one of the new-coined maxims of the times put it, to "let it all hang out". Little and even not so little girls go about dressed in '30s-style orphan Annie stocking, ripped and frayed mini skirts and turtle-neck sweaters, their arms covered in thin, silver, "hippy" bracelets and matching long earrings dangling from their ears - a look in its own way all rather pretentious, all quite kitsch.

The males, fighting their fathers all the way, follow a nouveau Edwardian style that includes waist-fitted, tailored jackets in coloured velvet with high necks and lacy shirts which are then worn with bell-bottom jeans. The smaller the boy, the wider the bells seem to get.

**165.** A 1980-style clown photographed while revelling at the Venice Carnival. The costume, no longer restricted to the essential outfit, now includes wig and elaborate make-up. Photo by courtesy of Alessandro Savella. 1984.

166.

## DESIGNER KIDS

The rebellion soon dies out, however, and several seasons later, round about the mid-'70s, the ready-made designer fashion craze for the very young breaks out.

**166.** During the seventies, kids' clothes mirror the rebellious spirit of many of their protestor-parents. The password: "Do your own thing". And the more eccentric the look - often imported from London - the better. The models: "Biba Baby & Co.". Photo by Richard Imrie, *Vogue Bambini*.

**167.170.** Again, we have London to thank for these rather bizarre but fun clothes that delight the kids and make them feel like little grown-ups, much in the same way as the classic styles of once upon a time did. Models: "Biba Baby & Co.". Photo by Richard Imrie, *Vogue Bambini*.

**168.169.** In the '70s, the whimsical may have the upper hand but the classically elegant is by no means dead and gone. Smocked and wide-skirted cotton muslins, velvets and taffetas are still around, as are the little white socks, the black patent-leather shoes and the classic good manners they're worn with. Photo by Paolo Poli.

166.

167.

168.

17

The first sector to be hit is that of knitwear and stretch fibers. But at the same time, these post-modern samurai of the ephemeral begin to dedicate their talents to the creation of high fashion for upper-class kids but end up dragging just about every class and age group into the act. Valentino, Armani, Krizia, Trussardi, Ferré, Barocco, Biagiotti, Coveri, Chicca Ruffini, Versace, Moschino and Fendi rule the chic, up market, fashion world. Fiorucci appeals to a more internationally, cosmopolitan, "ethnic" taste, inspired, as his fashions are, by popular dress all over the world.

For all the big name designers, creating "baby" and "junior" fashions becomes a must. As Krizia puts it, "The children's collections are what my imagination throws out first. It's upon these gay, fresh lines that I then work to come up with fashions for mother." A complete turn about from the time that kids wore miniature grown-up

169.

**171.172.** Christmas celebrations take on a more relaxed, casual air that is mirrored in the children's holiday fashions. At the same time however, the consumer society gets more demanding, fussier about its gifts and gastronomic treats, than ever before. Cake and candles with hot chocolate will no longer do. Now, it's got to be ice-cream, pastries, fruit drinks and coca-cola for our post-modern youth. Photo by Manfredi Bellati, *Vogue Bambini*.

styles, and that was simply the way things not only were, but simply had to be. In order to get the desired effect with the fabrics best suited to the new styles being created, designers and textile manufacturers join forces right from the start. The required fashion features for every occasion are now stretchability, practicality and softness.

Towards the end of the '70s the new order was pretty well established. Children could be said to rule the roost. They are spoiled and courted by society at large and the fashion industry in particular. For them a total look is created, a look that runs the gamut from their safety pins to the hats on their heads. Kids top the list of the consumers whose every wish is the fashion designers' command. They have become the biggest of the big spenders.

PRESS RELEASE

In 1977, *Vogue Bambini* formulates its new deference for this world dominated by children in a campaign for colour that could not fail to hit its mark. "The world is in

173. For his society appearances, this little boy chooses to dress like the grown-ups he'll be rubbing elbows with: a round-necked pullover, a starched white collar and a little red bow tie. Photo by Toni Meneguzzo, *Vogue Bambini*.

174. In similar circumstances, this little girl prefers a beginning-of-the-century, antique lace look that betrays its times only by virtue of its mini length. Photo by Manfredi Bellati, *Vogue Bambini*.

colour, especially the child's world. And all the colours of the rainbow have come back to settle just where they belong - on the child". The idea is a good one, if not exactly novel. It will suffice us to think of how Picasso liked to portray his child models in fancy dress.

And so we get great splashes of colour: red shorts worn with bright green knee socks, a bright yellow T-shirt, a blue over-shirt and cherry red canvas shoes and little girls in pumpkin sun dresses slipped over bright orange blouses. Hem-lines are once more below the knee and hair is worn straight and down to shoulder length. Krizia, who's been taking care of kids since 1969, can be considered an expert in the field. In these years she takes to designing light-hearted and festive, wide, multi-coloured striped overalls.

The popularity of jeans continues to go unrivalled but now, in addition to the classic

**175.**

**175. 176. 177.** The '80s bring changes to even the most traditional ceremonial dress. For modern First Communions, short dresses are also worn. Veils are out and simple straw hats or flower wreaths are in, as are long, straight, carefree hair styles. Photo by Paolo Poli; photos by Didier Massard, *Vogue Bambini*.

**176.**

**178.**

**179.**

**180.**

styles and brand names which continue to exist, these too have gone up market and become a concern of the fashion industry. A certain share of the jeans market is now "designer" and, consequently, expensive. These are the dress jeans, good for any occasion. Practically everybody from infancy on owns a pair of some kind of jeans, or two or more.

This is also a time of experimentation with new fabrics. New and better spot-proof, no-iron materials are created. We now have napless, downy surface, plush, teaseled cottons and the "stone-washed", faded fabrics, along with endless stretch fibres to meet the new and pressing demand for versatility.

Part of the new climate are the new publications like the monthly started up in '77, *Zero Sei*, ("Zero Six"), a magazine catering to fashions for kids from birth to the age of six. *Dalla parte delle bambine*, ("On the girls' side") comes out for the first time in the same year and has as its *raison d'être* the fostering of little girls' rights in the

**178.179.18O.** In the latter '70s, a quite definite touch of the romantic appears in children's party dress. Eighteenth century-style shirts and large, gauzy collars that are often embroidered and trimmed in *guipure* dress up the simplest knit dresses and velvet trousers. Photo by Toni Meneguzzo, *Vogue Bambini.*

face of the presumed domination of their male contemporaries and the education of these too-sweet young things to the necessity of fighting for those rights. Children's Fashion plus Feminism, so to speak.

## A WHIRL OF COLOUR

With the arrival of the 1980s, children's fashions continued to receive the attention of the big name designers, especially the Italian ones. The looks they come up with are ever more coordinated, total, varied according to the occasion and not necessarily prohibitive price-wise. The world is certainly a different one from that of the past. Gone are the fairy tale days of grandma's hand-knit sweaters and embroidery. In her place is an industry that "cares" for the child's every need, from his or her disposable diaper to outfits for those special occasions which, though often quite different from what they used to be, still continue to call for the "right" thing to wear. So baby is still pampered - indeed too much, according to some.

The styles of the late '80s move simultaneously along two parallel lines in search of the refined and the casual. The blue blazer has made a come back, adding a touch of classic, drawing-room elegance to the boys' outfits. It is cut short like the traditional spencer and made of light-weight, "cool" wool or linen in summer and heavier wool in winter. With it are worn long silk or flannel trousers, or even those of

181.

**181.** In the '80s, with the rebellious tide receding, classic party dress comes back into vogue once again. And yet, remnants of the gay and fancy-free seventies cannot help but remain. Photo by Marco Lanza, *Moda in Baby*, July-September, 1983.

**182.** Nicola Trussardi's little girl in neo-romantic guise. Photos by kind courtesy of N. Trussardi. 1988.

classic blue and deep-green plaid wool. The shirt is white or striped, depending on the occasion, while now the long or bow tie is more of a must than ever before.

For dressing up the girls, the white organdy or taffeta dress with embroidered yoke, puffed-sleeves and coloured sash around the waist is still a favorite and, if anything, even more decorated with lace and flounce than in the past, almost in assertion of the child's sacred right to carefree gaity. Side by side with these classics, new variations of traditional themes co-exist. Colors and fabrics are varied. Plaid dresses are livened up with little white collar and

**183.** The heights of elegance: one model by that famous Italian designer, Valentino. It's a velvet, lapel-less, single-button blazer worn with impeccable long, grey flannel trousers. Photo by Fiorenzo Niccoli, *Moda in Baby*, no. 2, 1982.

183.

182.

**184.185.** A new Spanish inventiveness also testifies to the recent return to traditional elegance. *El Corte Ingles,* 1988.

cuffs. Kids can choose from among delicate voile flower prints, op-art patterns, over-sized checks, new-style sailor suits and just about everything that could appeal to any fancy. As always, hem-lines rapidly go up and down but, like never before, practically anything goes, as long as it stays within the less rigidly defined but nonetheless always present boundaries of popular taste.

In any case, a point to be made is that what a child now wears for today's special occasions is the result of genuine and often intense two-way negotiations between the older and younger generations, when, that is, it is not simply imposed by the latter! Even the First Communion wear has undergone a minor transformation in recent years. Though the dress is still white, it is sometimes short and even those who opt for full length have put aside the traditional veil in preference for a simple wreath of flowers or straw hat. The boys refuse to give up their much-loved jeans even on this day and limit themelves to adding an elegant touch with a

186.

187.

1

blue blazer and a little bow tie. And the phenomenon is widespread-not least due to the fact that even in a time when anything goes, a child's instinct for emulation remains extremely strong. Consequently, although the permissive climate encourages them in theory to wear what they please, in reality they all choose what everyone else does. But the point is that *this* is what they please. And that means that little Tom Thumb has definitely taken some very giant steps in recent history, and not only in the realm of fashion.

As we noted above, this century was heralded as being that of the child. With very few reservations, it can be said that in the family and the field of education great strides have been made in safeguarding what are the inalienble rights of children. And these same rights have been the motivating force behind the spirit of play, of freedom and of the ephemeral which have slowly come to inspire the clothes our children dress up in, what we used to call their "Sunday Best". Perhaps that is why having them brought to mind now and again can be such a pleasure.

**186.** As we head towards the year 2000, the *broderie anglaise* look with its turn-of-the-century elegant simplicity is back in the child's dress code for those special occasions. Photo by Ray Jones, *Moda in Baby*, no. 12, 1985.

**187.** Laura Biagiotti's daughter, Lavinia, wears a "First Empire"-style dress in white linen batiste, embroidered with *entre-deux*: an original creation of her mom's. From Laura Biagiotti's private collection, photo by Michelotti.

**188.** Even the most perfect gentlemen wear plimsolls these days! Another saucy touch: his pink tie. Photo by Leonardo Maniscalchi, *Moda in Baby*, no. 13, 1985.

**189.**

**189.** Franco Moschino's ideal little girl: sweet and subtly demure. The long stockings, satin collar and big bow at the waist give the impression of a designer squarely facing the future, but with the past never too far from his mind. Photo: Fabrizio Ferri, by kind courtesy of the Moschino Studio. 1986.

# APPENDIX

# GLOSSARY

| ITALIANO | ENGLISH | FRANÇAIS | DEUTSCH |
|---|---|---|---|
| Arricciatura | **Curliness** | Fronces | Kräuseln |
| Balza | **Flounce** | Ruches | Rüschen |
| Bambina | **Girl** | Fillette | Mädchen |
| Bambino | **Baby boy** | Garçon | Knabe |
| Bambini | **Children** | Enfants | Kinder |
| Baschina | **Flap, basque** | Basque | |
| Batista | **Lawn, cambric** | Batiste | Batist |
| Blusa | **Smock** | Blouson | Kittel |
| Bretelle | **Braces, straps** | Bretelles | Träger |
| Calzamaglia | **Leotards** | Chausse | Strumpfhosen |
| Calzettoni | **Long socks** | Chaussette montant | Kniestrümpfe |
| Calzoni | **Breeches** | Culottes | Pumphose |
| Carnevale | **Carnival** | Carnaval | Fasching |
| Cintura | **Sash, waist band** | Ceinture | Gürtel |
| Compleanno | **Birthday** | Anniversaire | Geburtstag |
| Comunione | **First Communion** | Première communion | Erstekommunion |
| Corpetto | **Bodice** | Brassière, corsage | Leibchen |
| Cravatta | **Necktie** | Cravate | Kravatte |
| Cresima | **Confirmation** | Confirmation | Firmung |
| Damigella (d'onore) | **Bridesmaid** | Demoiselle d'honneur | Brautjungfer |
| Falpalà | **Furbelow** | Falbala | Falbel |
| Fiocco | **Bow** | Rosette | Schleife |
| Fodera | **Lining** | Doublure | Fütterung |
| Ghirlanda | **Garland** | Guirlande | Blumenkränzchen |
| Gonna | **Skirt** | Jupe | Rock |
| Grembiule | **Apron** | Tablier | Schürtze |
| Lutto | **Mourning** | Deuil | Traue |
| Manica | **Sleeve** | Manche | Ärmel |
| Manica a sbuffo | **Puffing sleeves** | Manche à gigot | Puffärmel |
| Mantello | **Cloak** | Manteau | Mantel |
| Marinara | **Sailorsuit** | Marinière | Matrosenanzug |
| Mascherata | **Fancy dress** | Deguisement | Vermummung |
| Matrimonio | **Wedding** | Mariage | Hochzeit |
| Merletto | **Lace** | Dentelle | Spitze |
| Minigonna | **Miniskirt** | Minijupe | Minirock |
| Organza | **Organdi** | Organdi | Organdin |
| Paggio | **Page** | Garçon d'honneur | Schleppenträger |
| Pagliaccetto | **Rompers** | Barboteuse | Strampelhose |
| Panno | **Cloth** | Drap | Tuch |
| Pantaloni | **Trousers, slacks** | Pantalon | Lange Hose |
| Pantaloni corti | **Shorts** | Shorts | Kurze Hose |
| Pantaloni alla zuava | **Knickerbockers** | Knickerbockers | Knickebockers |
| Paramani | **Cuffs** | Poignée | Ärmelaufschlag |
| Pullover | **Sweater** | Chandail | Pullover |
| Scamiciato | **Jumper** | Chasuble | Kleiderrock |
| Scozzese | **Tartan** | Ecossais | Schottenstoff |
| Sottogonna | **Petticoat** | Jupon | Unterrock |
| Stivaletto | **Bootee** | Bottines | Stiefelette |
| Tuta | **Overalls** | Salopette | Overall |

| ESPAÑOL | РУССКИЙ | 注 | 释 | |
|---|---|---|---|---|
| Fruncido | Завивка | ギャザー | 見せかけボタン | |
| | | | 絹帯 | |
| Volante | Оборка | すそのひだ飾り | パンタロンのボタン | |
| Niña | Девочка | 女の子 | ホック | |
| Niño | Мальчик | 男の子 | ショートパンツ | |
| Niños | Дети | 子供たち | ズボンつり | |
| Faldita | Берет | バスク | ゴムのズボンつり | |
| Batista | Батист | 麻上布 | 長ズボン．スラックス | |
| Blusa | Блуза | ブラウス | トルコふうズボン | |
| Tirantes | Подтяжки | ズボンつり | バルーンパンタロン | |
| | | | (ズボンの)股 | |
| Leotardo | Рейтузы, Колготки | タイツ | ファスナー |  |
| Calcetines | Гольфы | 厚手の長靴下 | ベルト | |
| Pantalones | Брюки | 長ズボン | パンタロンのベルト | |
| Carnaval | Карнавал | カーニヴァル | 見せかけの | |
| Cinturón | Пояс | バンド | 裏地 | |
| Cumpleaños | День рождения | 誕生日 | (ズボンの)裏打ち | |
| Comunión | Причащение | 聖体拝領式 | (ズボンの)足 | |
| Corpiño | Лиф, Корсаж | チョッキ | 靴カバー | |
| Corbata | Галстук | ネクタイ | キルティング、ステッチ | |
| Confirmación | Миропомазание | 堅信式 | ギャザー | |
| | | | パンタロン | |
| Damisela (de honor) | Фрейлина | 花嫁の付添い役の少女 | エレガントなパンタロン | |
| | | | ズアーヴパンツ | |
| Lechuguilla | Оборка | フリル | 七部丈のズボン |  |
| Nudo | Бант | 飾り結び | 直線立ちのパンタロン | |
| Forro | Подкладка | 裏地 | ラッパズボン | |
| | | | ショートパンツ | |
| Guirnalda | Венок | 花飾り | 乗馬用ズボン | |
| Falda | Юбка | スカート | 作業用ズボン | |
| Delantal | Передник, фартук | エプロン | 登山用スラックス | |
| | | | スキー用スラックス | |
| Luto | Траур, Траурное платье | 喪服 | 礼式用パンタロン | |
| | | | なめし皮のパンタロン | |
| Manga | Рукав | 袖 | 毛皮のパンタロン | |
| Manga ahuecada | Рукав с буфами | パフ・スリーブ | 伸縮性に富んだパンタロン | |
| Capa | Мантия, Манто | マント，ケープ | 夏用の薄手のパンタロン |  |
| Marinera | Матросская куртка | セーラー服 | コール天のパンタロン | |
| Disfraz | Маскарад | 仮装舞踏会 | 冬用のパンタロン | |
| Matrimonio | Свадьба | 結婚式 | スポーティなパンタロン | |
| Encaje | Кружева | レース | ひざ当て | |
| Minifalda | Миниюбка | ミニスカート | (バンドなどを通す)輪 | |
| | | | ズボンの折り目 | |
| Organdí | Органди | オーガンディ | ダーツ | |
| | | | (ズボンの裾の)折り返し | |
| Paje | Паж | 小姓 | パンタロンのポケット | |
| Pelele | Детский комбинезон | コンビネーション | 縁取りをしたポケット | |
| Paño | Сукно | ラシャ | パッチポケット | |
| Pantalones | Брюки, панталоны | パンタロン | 折り畳み式ポケット | |
| Pantalones cortos | Трусы | 半ズボン | 袋型の横ポケット |  |
| Knickerbockers | Гольфы | ニッカーホッカーズ | 台形型ポケット | |
| Puño | Обшлаг, отворот | 装飾用のそで口 | 尻ポケット | |
| Pullover | Свитер | セーター | 袋型のポケット | |
| | | | 袋型のポケット | |
| Jumper | Джемпер | ジャンパースカート | | |
| Escocés | Шотландка | 格子縞の織物 | 袋型で二重に縫ってある | |
| Enaguas | Нижняя юбка | ペチコート | ポケット | |
| Botita | Высокий ботинок | 半長靴 | トラックスーツ |   |
| | | | コーデュロイ、コール天 | |
| Mono | Комбинезон | トラックスーツ | | |

# BIBLIOGRAPHY

126

## BOOKS

1949 - D. Macardle, *Children of Europe*, Ed. Gollanez, London

1955 - A. Allen, *The Story of Clothes*, Faber and Faber, London

1961 - M. Vicino, *Storia del costume*, Ist. Poligrafico dello Stato, Roma

1962 - U. Fragola, *L'intervento dei pubblici poteri nel settore della moda in Italia*, Istituto della Stampa, Napoli

1964 - R. Levi-Pisetzky, *Storia del costume in Italia*, Ist. Editoriale Italiano, Milano

1970 - L. Kibalowa, O. Herbenowa, M. Lamarova, *Encyclopédie illustrée du costume*, Gründ, Paris.

1972 - A. Sandre, *Storia del costume*, Edizioni d'Arte, Torino

1975 - S. Agnelli, *Vestivamo alla marinara*, Mondadori, Milano

1976 - A. Philippe, *Padri e figli nell'Europa medioevale e moderna*, Laterza, Roma-Bari

1976 - J. Robinson, *Arte e moda nel '900*, Ist. Geografico De Agostini, Novara

1977 - E. Ewing, *History of Children's Costume*, B.T. Batsford, London

1977 - AA.VV. *Storia dell'industria italiana*, Etas Libri, Milano

1979 - G. Dorfles, *Mode e Modi, la ricerca iconografica*, Mazzotti, Milano

1979 - *Pariser Mode vor hundert Jahren*, Harenberg Kommunikation, Dortmund

1979 - R. Pistolese, *La moda nella storia del costume*, Cappelli, Bologna

1981 - G. Butazzi, *Moda Arte Storia e Società*, Fabbri, Milano

1981 - M.A. Descamps, *Psicologia della Moda*, Ed. Riuniti, Roma

1982 - N. Aspesi, *Il lusso e l'autarchia*, Rizzoli, Milano

1982 - N. Calandri, *Storia e favole di moda*, Alinari, Firenze

1984 - A.Jarvis and P. Raine, *Fancy dress*, Shire Publication, Aylesbury